The **Dog**Guardian

YOUR GUIDE TO A HAPPY, WELL-BEHAVED DOG

NIGEL REED

The **Dog** **Guardian**

Contents

About the Author 7

Introduction 14

PART 1
History And Ideas

Chapter 1   The Canine Journey 19

Chapter 2   Training Models...................................... 31

PART 2
The Method

Chapter 3   Your Dog's Needs.................................... 49

Chapter 4   Your Dog's Language.............................. 71

Chapter 5   Your Dog's State 97

Chapter 6   Leadership 112

PART 3
Case Studies

Chapter 7   Issues With Food................................... 137

Chapter 8   Dogs and Perceived Dangers 141

Chapter 9   Dogs That Do Not Get On With Each Other... 153

Chapter 10   Attention-Seeking Behaviours............ 156

Chapter 11   Rough Play 165

Chapter 12   Separation Anxiety 168

Chapter 13   The Walk – On Lead 172

Chapter 14   The Walk – Off Lead 179

Chapter 15   Obsessive Behaviours.. 184

Chapter 16   Toilet Issues 187

Chapter 17   Nervous Behaviours.. 191

Chapter 18   Double Trouble.. 197

Chapter 19   Managing Other People 201

Chapter 20   Dogs and Children.. 204

Chapter 21   Puppies 210

Chapter 22   A Realisation 220

Afterword 229

Acknowledgements 231

References... 233

About the Author

When I was a child on my way to school each morning, I'd pass a house where a beautiful Corgi called Misty lived. Misty would be lying down in the garden, watching the schoolchildren walk past. Once she saw me approaching, she would get up and push her nose through the gate, and wag her tail to coax me into petting her. I'd routinely sit on the floor and stroke her for as long as I could before having to rush to school to make it on time. My meetings with Misty were my favourite part of the day, and the time when I first discovered my love for dogs.

Because of being in awe of Misty, I asked my parents if we could get a dog. They gave it some serious thought, as they knew how much it would mean to me, but decided against it, as the responsibility of caring for the dog would have fallen on them, and they worked too many hours to give it the attention it needed. I was devastated by their decision but looking back, I know they made the right choice.

To compensate for not growing up with dogs at home, I would regularly seek out canine company. In particular, I grew very fond of my neighbour's dog, called Kenny, who I'd take out for long walks in Cornwall where I lived. When I approached my neighbour's house, Kenny would pick up my scent through the door and start barking with excitement. There were times when he was left at home alone; he'd manage to escape out of a window and make his way to my house to come and see me. In the summer, we would go to the beach and I'd watch him run excitedly in and out of the sea whilst the sun sparkled off the water. As I felt the heat on my skin, I could hear the sound of waves gently crashing on the beach.

In these moments, I felt at total peace with the world and wanted for nothing but what I had in front of me.

In my early twenties, I chose to follow my love of dogs by working with them as a career. I began learning about their behaviour from many different experts, via books, TV, attending talks and enrolling on courses. I began piecing together the jigsaw puzzle of dog behaviour and good ownership by adopting communication and nurturing ideas that were kind and effective, and dismissing the unkind and quick-fix ones. Once I achieved the necessary certificates, qualifications and knowledge to become a dog behaviourist, I started helping owners address their dogs' undesirable issues on the weekends, with varying degrees of success.

As I gained more experience, I realised one of the major factors to helping dogs was down to the way that information was presented to their owners, as it was them, after all, who needed to be empowered to get the results. So I began reading books on human psychology, parenting and coaching. Whilst reading these books, I picked up lots of invaluable information and stumbled across a huge piece of the dog behavioural jigsaw puzzle. I was amazed this information was not common practice, considering how important it was to the dog's wellbeing. I gathered this information with what I had previously learnt to form a kind, effective, holistic approach to dog ownership that people could easily understand.

In my late twenties, I moved to London to work with dogs full time. Since the move, I have worked with hundreds of clients and their dogs, all over Britain and Europe. I've been regularly featured on the radio and have written many behavioural advice articles for dog magazines. Through my experiences with dogs, I've come across a wide spectrum of behaviours from many breeds, and difficult situations with varied attitudes from the owners, all of which have further shaped my learning. I have encountered some extremely tough cases, but I am yet to meet a dog with behavioural issues that couldn't be helped; the owner just needed guidance, the right information and to possess the necessary determination. I hope to give you these things via this book and the free accompanying videos (details of which can be found in the Afterword), online and in-person courses, consultations, talks and my blog: for more on this, see my website: www.thedogguardian.com.

I have given myself a goal to help better the life of 100,000 dogs in my lifetime, and I cannot complete this goal without you. So I invite you to join me on a journey to achieve the perfect relationship with your dog and to share your story through my Facebook page and YouTube account. I look forward to hearing your own unique story very soon.

Introduction

Dogs are a gift to us.

They are loyal companions, trusted allies and part of the family all rolled into one. We go to great lengths to provide for our furry friends. We invite them into our homes, feed, protect and care for them. However, despite us living side by side with dogs for thousands of years, they are still very much misunderstood.

Imagine living in a world you can't make sense of, where the rules constantly change. A world where the people you live with do not speak your language and you can't distinguish a friend from an enemy. Imagine potential threats coming at you every day and your loved ones are looking to you for protection. And in return for putting your life on the line for them, imagine that you get punished, abandoned or suffer a worse fate. You've just put yourself in the mind of millions of dogs around the world.

Every dog desperately wants to be understood by their human family so they're able to relax and enjoy their life. Unfortunately, there are countless scenarios where this is not the case. These dogs exhibit a wide range of behavioural problems – from pulling on the lead and not listening when called, to aggression and nervousness. These problems put the relationship under strain, and are unpleasant for all involved.

Many dedicated owners seek to address problematic behaviour with corrective techniques sourced from books, television, the internet, dog trainers, family and friends. Yet despite their best efforts, even the most experienced of dog owners can meet a particularly challenging case and fail in their mission.

Those who manage to correct their dog's problem behaviour often do so by distracting or controlling it with the aid of a gadget, or through excessive exercise. But what if there was something important we were all missing? What if there was a more effective approach that would allow us to listen and communicate with our dogs on a much deeper level?

The purpose of this book is to help you achieve the perfect relationship with your dog. It is a narrative that reveals the key principles to securing your dog's wellbeing. This information will empower you in your role as guardian to ensure your dog is happy, well-behaved and looks to you for guidance.

The Dog Guardian begins by examining how the dog has evolved from its wolf ancestors to live with us in our homes. This is significant because understanding the evolution process helps us understand the core principles of canine nature, language and hierarchy.

We then look at the different ways to train a dog. There are generally two schools of thought. One side relies on stimulus response training and believes an understanding of wolf behaviour has next to no relevance in understanding domestic dogs. The other side believes an understanding of wolf behaviour is crucial to understanding a dog's motivation. Each side has their own ideas, theories and practices that appear to get results, but there are misunderstandings on both sides.

The side that dismisses wolf pack hierarchy ideas uses a variety of techniques, including positive and negative reinforcement, and conditioning methods to address undesirable behaviour. Using these techniques often results in failing to explore the reasons behind this behaviour.

On the other side are those who have seriously misinterpreted how wolf behaviour can translate to dogs in our home life. These errors are mainly due to people seeing aggressive wolf behaviour as a justification to use force when 'training' their dogs. This backward philosophy has caused many to distance themselves from any wild canine comparisons. As a result, terms such as 'alpha', 'pack leader' and 'dominance' have become very unpopular with some. In this book, I hope to explain how the thinking has come about on both sides and how we can move on from this.

We then examine the core factors in securing our dog's wellbeing: the dog's needs and the owner's role as fulfiller of needs. Popular belief teaches us what our dogs need and what we must do each day to fulfil them. However, in *The Dog Guardian*, we use a hierarchical model of needs, which is a different model from current practice. This model will shed new light on the motivation behind a dog's behaviour by identifying what is most important for the dog at the time. Once you know exactly what your dog needs and how important those needs are in each moment, it creates a deeper understanding and a stronger bond between you and your dog. This knowledge could potentially save you thousands of misdirected training hours of turmoil and stress, when all that is needed is a simple change of mindset. Identifying the dog's needs is very important because unfulfilled needs are the root cause of all undesirable behaviour.

Communication is crucial to the relationship between humans and dogs, and this book looks at how the dog can misinterpret its role, believing it is responsible for fulfilling its own and the family's needs. Problems then arise, as a dog is not capable of fulfilling its own needs in a human world, resulting in undesirable behaviour, ranging from the subtle to the dramatic.

Observing how wild canines interact with one another gives us a deep insight into how they have managed to communicate and understand each other's intentions for millions of years. We translate this language into step-by-step instructions so you can successfully communicate with your dog. And once you achieve that, you can reinforce the message that *you* are the needs fulfiller. In turn, your dog will look to you for information regarding its needs in each area of its life. Once your dog can assess your reactions and trust your decisions, it is reassured about the world around it – and behavioural problems disappear.

Next, we examine how the environment can affect a dog's emotional state of mind to trigger undesirable behaviour. This information will allow you to identify your dog's emotional state by reading the signals that convey its concerns. By correctly identifying what affects your dog's state, you will be empowered with a course of action to avoid and interrupt these experiences, and instead, plan a series of positive experiences to ensure the dog's confidence grows in every situation. This involves three elements: planning what your dog is subjected to, and ensuring a series of positive experiences; making quick decisions to avoid a rise in your dog's anxiety; and using techniques to reduce your dog's state if anxiety does rise. These steps will reinforce your position as an effective decision-maker, whilst also teaching your dog self-control.

This means we need to examine our leadership style, management of situations and mindset, all of which are very important because it is ultimately our actions that make the difference between falling at the first hurdle and tackling the most difficult cases. This book explains how to do this by identifying good leadership traits, and suggesting how to manage home life so your dog has many positive lessons and experiences. Ultimately, this will build their trust in you and strengthen your relationship.

Sharing my clients' cases will reinforce the information in this book. These cases delve deeper into behavioural problems and how they can be overcome. I have had many experiences of both working with dogs on their own and guiding owners in how to address their dogs' undesirable behaviours. In my work, I have encountered setbacks and experienced struggles. But the success of each story demonstrates how the dog has taught both the owner and myself valuable lessons in becoming good leaders by mastering canine language; in each case, only when the owner and I got the communication right did the dog follow.

My hope is that by using this book, you can build a happier and more fulfilling relationship with your dog, based on understanding, trust and effective leadership.

PART 1
HISTORY AND IDEAS

Chapter 1
The Canine Journey

"According to Darwin's Origin of Species, it is not the most intellectual of the species that survives; it is not the strongest that survives; but the species that survives is the one that is able best to adapt and adjust to the changing environment in which it finds itself." (Leon C. Megginson)

In the beginning

Our love for dogs has allowed their numbers to flourish all around the world, as we invite them into our homes and feed, care and provide for them. It is clear they would not be around in their existing numbers today if we hadn't joined forces; but it is even speculated that many of *us* would not be here today if it weren't for their help.

They have acted as guards for our protection, hunters to help us get food, and herders for our livestock. We have crime-fighting police dogs, guide dogs to help the blind, and rescue dogs to save lives. And for most of us, they act as companions, giving us unconditional love and thus, fulfilling our human needs.

But our relationship was not always like this, so just how did it all begin?

Origins of the canine

The path to the modern-day dog started 55 to 60 million years ago in the form of the Miacids. Miacids were small, tree-dwelling animals with long tails and bodies, which lived on a diet of small animals and insects. They were split into two groups: viverravines and vulpavines. Both varieties of Miacid would prove to be extremely adaptable over their next evolutionary stages.

The viverravines became hunters, using ambushing techniques and stealth to take down prey, and evolved into felines. The vulpavines had an amazing ability to adapt to available food and weather conditions: a huge evolutionary advantage that allowed them to inhabit nearly every environment. They eventually evolved into canines.

Around 20 million years later, the dawn dog (or Hesperocyon) evolved from the vulpavines. Its teeth were not like the cat's sabre teeth, but were instead all set inside its muzzle. No longer a tree-dwelling animal, the dawn dog had a low body and lengthy tail, allowing it to move quickly in the undergrowth. Its diet consisted of small animals, and so did not require it to live in large packs to take down prey, but with the help of a mate, the dawn dog could claim territory and defend it.

Over the next two million years, the descendants of the dawn dogs evolved into two main groups that inhabit the planet today: lupines (wolf-like) and vulpines (foxes).

The evolution of prey such as antelope and zebra led to the lupines' need to unite in order to successfully catch their prey. As the lupines collaborated, their communication skills around food, hunting, protection, status and bringing up the young developed to form a co-operative group. By comparison, foxes continued to find small prey and so became solitary hunters that do not need to possess such a large repertoire of interspecies communication.

Over time, the success of pack formation for the lupines allowed the species to thrive and emerge into the variations we see today, such as the coyote and the formidable grey wolf.

The wolf pack formation

Wolves form packs for their best chance at survival, as they are all faced with the daily struggle of starvation, risk of injury, and acquiring and holding onto territory. Their environment is hostile and unforgiving, with the average life expectancy a mere four years. Wolves are dependent on a strong, solid unit, with two animals in charge: the alpha male and female. It is this pair's responsibility to fulfil the pack's needs.

The pack is often made up of a breeding pair and their offspring, but it can become more complex, adapting its membership by any means necessary in order to survive; for example, in more secluded environments, wolves may allow foreign members to breed with a pack member to ensure genetic diversity.

Wolf communication

Wolves have evolved to master a wide range of communication skills. These cover social status, as well as expressing feelings and mood. They also convey a complex array of information through a variety of methods, including observation, play and interaction. Communication for wolves and dogs alike is three-dimensional and varied, entailing *sight*, *touch*, *sound*, *scent* and *taste*.

touch
taste
sound
scent
sight

Language

When communicating, wolves will use their bodies to convey alertness, anger, fear, defensiveness, aggression, suspicion, relaxation, tension, happiness, fondness, playfulness, hunting, and occupied territory, using all five senses.

Visual communication

They will use posture and gestures, facial expressions, eyes, ears, teeth, lips, forehead, eyebrows, torso, tail, and stance to demonstrate status and mood, and so display a multitude of signals – to back off or approach for play, for instance.

Touch

Touch can be used for friendly behaviour, affection and interaction with the pack. It reduces levels of stress and is necessary for the pups' development. Touch may also be used in ritualised fighting, courtship and play, or as a last resort to address heated situations.

Sounds

There are a variety of sounds used by wolves, including:

- *Barking – to alert the rest of the pack that they're in imminent danger.*
- *Whimpering/whining – to show submission or pain.*
- *Growling/snarling – to let others know to back off.*
- *Howling – to call back separated pack members, or to let rival packs know of their presence. Some biologists believe wolves howl to express happiness and to mourn the death of other pack members.*

Smell

The wolf's sense of smell, being so much greater than a human's, has a multitude of uses, including:

- *To identify the sex, status, age and health of another of the species.*
- *To locate food/prey, danger, rivals and territory. It is speculated that wolves use scent-rolling to hide their natural smell for hunting purposes.*
- *To mark territory to send the message to neighbouring wolf packs that the area is occupied.*

Taste

Little is known about wolves communicating with taste, as the behaviour can easily be confused with their natural scent abilities. It is understood that, although they can distinguish between the four major groups of taste – sweet, sour, bitter and salty – they have less than a quarter of the taste receptors on their tongues that humans have.

Wolf language is often subtle and can be used to settle pack conflicts before they become serious disputes, without wasting too much energy, much like an apology or an acknowledgment can in our own language. Wolves can use aggression in heated situations, but aggression is a small part of wolf life, whereas day-to-day bonding and the responsibility of fulfilling the pack's needs play a huge part (television documentaries often show aggression over bonding to make the programmes more compelling). Wolves invest much time in nurturing and preparing their young with the skills needed to help the pack survive.

Wolves are not only strong and fit but they are also extremely competent at working together within the pack, which would otherwise become dysfunctional and would not survive. It is, however, ultimately the leaders who are responsible for the pack's survival. If they do not fulfil this role then the pack's needs are not being met, and the other pack members could die from starvation or attack, or during the hunt. So it is vital that the leaders are suitable for the job. The subordinates will observe their leaders' competency in the role and, depending on the pack structure, may leave, or in some cases, even challenge the leaders for the role.

Pack life is complicated and diverse, and can resemble a soap opera, with its sibling disputes, unauthorised offspring pregnancies, friendships and fallouts. We share common ties with the wolf, its family life and its bonds. Perhaps, with all of these similarities, this is the foundation of why we widely accept the dog as a friend.

From wolf to dog

Exactly when, where and how the dog evolved from its wild ancestor has been in debate for many years by evolutionary scientists. The origins of domestication occurred somewhere between 12 and 50,000 years ago. There is no definitive answer as it is hard to pinpoint exactly when it occurred for a couple of reasons, one being that dogs may have evolved from wolves in different regions in the world at similar times. The other reason is that scientists were previously looking for the physical changes that occurred from wolf to dog, whereas the domestication process was primarily a psychological change. The dog most certainly looked like a wolf for many years. Native Americans, for example, did not selectively breed their dogs, which consequently maintained their wolf aesthetics.

Studies on where domestication happened have pointed to Europe, the Middle East, China, and now most recently, Central Asia.

How the dog became a domesticated animal is also the subject of many theories, including wolves becoming tame because of lingering around the outskirts of villages for scraps of food when people abandoned their meals. Biologist Raymond Coppinger believed that these wolves would have had a decreased flight distance (the distance a wild animal keeps between itself and perceived danger), and as a result, they would have slowly become used to human activity and domesticated themselves. Over time, they would breed and the pups would be more socialised to human interaction; and so the wolf evolved to befriend the human. Another theory involves early socialisation of found puppies. The theory goes that we found them, fed them and nurtured them into tame wolves.

There is, however, a big difference between a tame and a domesticated animal. Taming an animal involves conditioning it to become used to human company, whereas the domestication process involves the altering of the animal's genes, resulting in the animal wanting and needing human company to survive.

Raymond Coppinger states that even tamed wolves aren't likely to be docile when it comes to food or breeding. He explains: '*I work with tamed wolves all the time. I don't care how tame they are, try to take their bone away. It's even worse when it comes to breeding. You start to fool around with wolves when they're in a courtship performance, you could die right there on the spot.*' In both accounts, early socialisation may tame a wolf around humans but it will not domesticate it.

In an attempt to find clues as to how the domestication from wolf to dog may have happened, scientists in Russia organised a breeding experiment with silver foxes. The aim was to see the behavioural, biological and physical changes that would occur as a result of human conditioning and attempted domestication. A study lasting over forty years showed adaptation responses and physiological variations that occurred within six generations as a result of human interference and an absence of natural selection. The results were of great interest. They produced phenotype variations similar to domestic dogs, such as floppy ears, colour changes, shorter/curled tails, altered skull dimensions and abnormal underbites (like the bulldog's), as well as a biological change in the foxes' oestrus cycles, in which a few females would have two annual cycles like the dog. They possessed juvenile characteristics and would whine, lick and try to get human attention. It is thought that these traits, if possessed by canines in the wild, would be a weakness and they would not have not survived.

A study led by geneticist Kerstin Lindblad-Toh at Uppsala University in Sweden (published in *Nature* online magazine) reveals that wolves first became domesticated by eating scraps of human food, which led to the positive selection of a genetic mutation allowing the digestion of starch, which has subsequently been added to the dog's genes but is missing in the wolf's. Another study (published in *PLoS Genetics*) suggests that dogs did not evolve from the modern-day wolf but a more closely-related wolf ancestor that is now extinct.

There are still many questions left to answer regarding just when, where and how the split happened, but many scientists agree on why humans and canines joined forces: to better fulfil their own needs for survival. Once the relationship evolved, it was mutually beneficial, as wolves benefited from a steadier food supply and the use of our weapons to take down prey, increasing their chances of living longer. Wolves helped to protect us and find and drive game, with their superior tracking abilities and speed.

The years that have passed

The wolf is an aloof animal, one that instinctively rejects human company, so the domestication process would involve selectively breeding from the ones that displayed the most social traits toward humans, allowing us to work together to achieve the same objectives.

In a pack of wild wolves, or many other canine packs, it is usually the leaders that breed to ensure only the best characteristics are passed on to the next generation, to keep the species strong and avoid overpopulating. When cohabiting with people, however, this wasn't the case. The wolf – or more accurately, as the evolution process took hold, the wolfdog – attached itself to a consistent food supply, and so breed control was not enforced.

The wolfdogs' appearance subsequently changed because natural selection was no longer a predominant factor. They now had us to help keep them alive. As a result, their brains and jaws were not put to the test daily, as they would have been in order to take down elk and other large prey on their own, and their natural strength was no longer needed to survive. This, along with the changing environment, the absence of controlled breeding, and food being more abundant, affected their behaviour. Their motivations changed, which resulted in different forms of communication, such as howling subsiding due to not needing to call back separated members, and adapting their barking to alert us to dangers and to get attention. The dog's need to claim a large territory in which its prey lived diminished over the years, but it is still a present instinct, as demonstrated with its reaction to an 'intruder'.

Through the years, a weaker but tamer companion was eventually created: the dog. It went from survival of the fittest to survival of the most co-operative.

As our journey together continued, inbreeding was actively practised to design dogs that were suitable for the jobs we had in mind. People with dogs would see the benefits of certain changes that were happening over time, and would then selectively breed from those animals in order to maintain certain traits. Some were bred to have thick coats to keep them warm in colder climates, whilst others were bred to have small bodies so they could fit down holes too small for humans.

The German Shepherd, for example, had to be big but not too heavy to be quick, and had to be alert and trainable. Breeders wanted a highly-intelligent dog that was not just capable of responding to the handler but also of thinking for itself when working with a flock. It had to be able to stand up to a ram but not alarm it by making too much noise or attacking the sheep.

Selective breeding over the last 50 years has mainly been for aesthetic purposes, to fit specific shapes and sizes for companionship, rather than for their function. The majority of dogs we have now are not usually used for their original purposes of protection, hunting and herding, etc., and generally have a different role: that of a companion, offering unconditional love.

Dogs in our homes

During the evolution from wolf to dog, many environmental changes and physical changes to the dog have occurred. These changes have only enhanced the dog's need to attach itself to a human to gain food, shelter and protection in order to survive.

In return for providing for their needs, we are blessed with a non-judgemental, loyal friend who truly appreciates us. Dogs regularly display their appreciation with affection, love, patience, and their willing-to-please attitude.

Their enthusiasm for life is a joy to observe. Their company brightens our days by making our walks fun and our evenings cosy. They regularly make us laugh as they unknowingly pull faces, thump us with their tails, and manage to have fun in seemingly boring situations. They break down social barriers as they compel total strangers to smile and talk to us. The mere sight of them can turn our sadness into smiles, anger into acceptance, and seriousness into play. Living with a dog also has proven health benefits, as our blood pressure decreases when we stroke them, and they motivate us to exercise more. The overall positive effect they have on our wellbeing cannot be measured.

Once the human and dog attachment forms, in many cases, we have a happy, well-behaved dog that fits in with our lives. However, there are also many situations in which dogs don't behave quite as we want them to – from pulling on the lead and not coming back to us when we call them, to confused, frightened, overexcited, nervous or aggressive behaviour. This puts the relationship under strain. Both human and dog want a peaceful life together, but problem behaviours exist due to a lack of understanding.

Chapter 2
Training Models

"We are drowning in information but starved for knowledge." (John Naisbitt)

There have been many theories from dog trainers, scientists and owners on the most effective ways to correct a dog's undesirable behaviour. The theories have divided people's opinions for many years and exhibit a wide variety of techniques such as positive reinforcement, negative consequence, force, distraction, associative learning, the use of gadgets and tools, and many others.

With all the different advice from television programmes, books, the internet and other dog owners, it has become very difficult to determine the most effective approach. This is in part due to proven 'results' attached to all the theories, with many people using similar methods but giving them different interpretations. All theories have one thing in common: they are all aimed at stopping undesirable behaviour and creating new, desirable habits.

Typically, the training models of dog behaviour fall into two categories: top-down and bottom-up. The top-down model is a study of behaviour as it was in the wild. This seeks to find an explanation for natural behaviour and examines the dog's changes in the context of environment and evolution. This can be a confusing study due to the many influences that affect behaviour in each situation.

The bottom-up approach is based on using corrective techniques but does not always incorporate environmental conditions and the dog's nature. In both these models, there are many practices and ideas that carry a different perspective. Each model has valuable information that can help us better understand dogs.

Learned behaviours

Perhaps the most well-known technique that assists in training dogs was discovered by the Russian physiologist, Ivan Pavlov. Pavlov noticed that dogs would salivate when an assistant entered the room with food. However, one day, he noticed that the dogs also salivated when the assistant entered without any food, and so it occurred to him that this response might not be down to a physiological process. Pavlov began further experiments to see if salivation was a learned response, using an unassociated stimulus – in this case, the sound of a bell, which he rang every time food was served. After many conditioning experiments with the bell and food, Pavlov discovered that the dogs would salivate on hearing the bell, and hence, that dogs can become conditioned to a response. Pavlov's conditioning techniques are a valuable tool in training, especially for police, assistance and rescue dogs.

Another experiment into dog behaviour was conducted by Seligman and Maier in the 1960s, in which two groups of dogs were introduced to a pain stimulus in the form of an electric shock. The first group could stop the stimulus by depressing a lever, but for the second group, the lever did nothing. Once the dogs had been conditioned, the researchers continued the experiment by putting each group into a large box with two compartments separated by a low wall in the middle. On one side of the wall, the dog would get a shock, but on the other, it would be safe, and the dog could easily jump over the wall to the side free from pain. The first group of dogs, who depressed the lever in the first experiment, had learned that their actions could influence the outcome; that is, that they could easily escape pain by jumping over the wall. The second group, however, somewhat surprisingly, just lay where they were, whining. Earlier in the experiment, the lever did nothing to alleviate the pain, so the dogs believed it was going to happen regardless of whether they jumped the wall or not, and they figured – why bother? In this group, the dogs had learned helplessness to a situation.

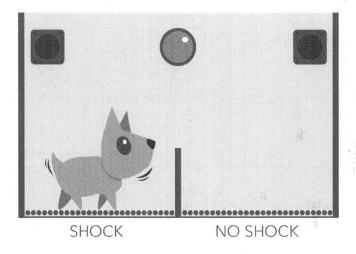

SHOCK   NO SHOCK

Understanding conditioning responses and how patterns of behaviour form from a bottom-up approach is very useful, but they do not tell us everything about the dog's needs, nature and psychology, or its relationships with others.

Correcting without questioning

As many training practices in each model appear to achieve results, it is just as important to ask why they are working as it is how to address behaviour. The dog-training market promotes an abundance of different training techniques that encourage owners to control, distract, mask or redirect problem behaviour rather than actually address it. For example, using force can appear effective in stopping a dog's undesirable behaviour, but this is a costly victory. A forceful owner may expect the dog to be obedient and conform to their commands, but an obedient dog is not necessarily a happy dog. If a dog bites back in a situation in which it was being forcefully confronted, I would consider that a natural reaction, whereas the forceful owner may have the animal put down for not being co-operative. The nature of the canine is good, or at least neutral, and not intrinsically evil. Undesirable behaviours are secondary reactions that occur from these incidents, and are natural under the circumstances. Punishing the dog rather than respecting their nature will produce more problems than it will settle. As the saying goes, 'If force is the answer then you are asking the wrong question'. Any lesson that involves force or confrontation cannot be practised safely for the dog or the person, and so should not even be an option.

The common forms of training that fail to deal with the issue behind the behaviour can be highlighted with an example of a dog that is terrified when visitors encroach on its territory, and consequently barks to get rid of them. Traditional dog-training solutions to these types of problems include demanding the dog to sit in a stern voice when people approach, which is a form of control, or instructing each visitor to give the dog food on their arrival (as I saw recently on a television programme). Each of these tactics to silence the dog may appear to 'work'. The technique that uses negative reinforcement to control (or even intimidate) the dog when someone comes to the door may see success in the form of the dog abiding by the command. Or the technique that uses positive reinforcement, with a stranger arriving at the door and rewarding the dog, will build a new neural association for the dog regarding what the presence of strangers means, leading to positive behaviour.

But both scenarios do not address the core issue – why does the dog feel it is necessary to protect the house in the first place? Why was it so stressed?

The list of techniques continue: many people use a head collar to stop a dog pulling on the lead, a spray collar to stop them barking, or a shock collar to stop them fighting. The term for this practice is *reductionism*; that is, seeing a problem and then looking for a solution. But with all the varied environmental factors to consider, the problem is smoothed over rather than properly addressed.

When we look at how to address our dogs' behavioural issues, there are many quick-fix 'solutions'. But trying to address a problem without understanding why the behaviour is happening can be detrimental to a dog's wellbeing, much like punishing a person without knowing the whole story. Putting someone in prison for stealing may address the crime, but it is important to identify their motivation for doing it in the first place. If the crime was committed by a drug addict, for example, there would be a deeper issue that needs addressing. Equally, a shock collar may temporarily control a dog, but it does not take into account its needs and what it is trying to say. If we look at the issue as a whole, we can learn to understand the reasons behind the behaviour.

Top-down thinking

To examine the top-down model of animal behaviour, it is necessary to understand evolution (Ádám Miklósi) and the drives and instincts the wolf needed to ensure its survival for as long as possible. The dogs' behaviours all stemmed from their wild counterparts, and changes then occurred through domestication, environmental influence and selective breeding. The dogs that were bred for working purposes were bred with an understanding of the canine's natural instincts, and worked with their social traits to reach a human goal. For example, the Border Collie was bred to herd, which came from the canine trait of pushing their prey forward to spot a physical weakness. Their natural behaviour was redirected to teach the dogs to round up rather than kill. Much has changed in their evolutionary journey, but understanding their nature gives us many clues to working with the domesticated dog.

The study of animals in their natural environment produces the purest subjects for the study of the language of any animal, but removed from the wild, they will adapt and develop new behaviours to cope with different pressures. As a result, their language and behaviour is muddled, which creates a confused picture. So, for example, studying wolves in a wolf park (a sanctuary for wolves) identifies different behaviour than that in their natural surroundings because they cannot leave.

In the wild, wolves need a leader to steer the subordinates, so there is a clear chain of command to provide food, protection and guidance. They are responsible for the wellbeing of the pack, and make the crucial decisions each day. In our home life together, the scenario is similar; the dog also needs a leader to provide food, protection and guidance, and assesses whether the owners are communicating their rightful role as leader. If the message as to who is in charge is confused, through either perceived weakness or miscommunication, the dog will have no choice but to assume the leadership role itself.

A dog that attempts to fulfil a leader's role and responsibilities will be out of its depth in terms of capability and understanding of its environment. The dog is not equipped to do this job in a world it does not understand. The confused behaviour resulting from trying to maintain a leadership position in this alien setting manifests itself in many erratic ways, such as separation anxiety, attacking strangers, either in the home or outside, obsessive behaviours, attacking other dogs, self-mutilation, constant barking, persistent following, pulling on the lead, defecating in the house, jumping up, ignoring requests, running away, chewing furniture, hyperactivity – the list is endless.

It should not be the dog's job to fulfil the role of leader and have the responsibilities that come with that position; it is our job as the guardian to make the big decisions, as we understand our environment. If we show the dog that we are worthy leaders by stepping up to the role then the dog will be relieved of those responsibilities and will trust in our leadership. Then we can have a happy, stress-free dog that can operate within the human environment without any anxiety. As a result, when a situation arises, the dog will look to us, as the more experienced member of its pack, for the appropriate reaction. When we have proved ourselves worthy and responded by remaining calm, to show that the situation is nothing to worry about, the dog in turn will think 'if they are fine then I must be fine, as they are in charge and the ones to be trusted'.

A human being leader does not mean that the dog will be unable to make any decisions or will be perfectly behaved all the time. Much like in the relationship between wolf parents and their litters, human parents and their children, or bosses and their workers, the less experienced members will occasionally question a leader's capabilities and authority, and may step out of line. But it is the leader's confident response and actions that will reconfirm the natural order. The followers will always have non-crucial decisions to make, but by leading effectively, the dog will trust in and look to you for major decisions regarding their needs for food, safety and wellbeing. And in turn, they will behave in a relaxed and happy manner.

Mixed opinions

The top-down philosophy is criticised by some who believe the dog in our homes is too far removed from its original form in the wild to make comparisons. Some authors reject the concept, making statements such as 'dogs are not wolves; you wouldn't look at monkey parenting to understand human parenting'. Whilst this statement has some *literal* truth, it insinuates that nothing can be learnt from a top-down study and thus, is rather misleading. This is because, whereas monkeys and humans are different species that evolved from a common ancestor, dogs are a subspecies of the wolf.

The dog, unlike the human and monkey, can breed, cohabit, produce fertile offspring, and communicate with the wolf, with a clear understanding of each other's language. The Saarloos Wolfhound and Czech Wolfdog are living proof, and strictly employing the above statement in one's thinking would mean completely discounting canine nature and millions of years of inbuilt behaviours. To extend the monkey/human parenting analogy, I also believe a third model can be used: **anthropomorphising dog training**. This model involves reflecting on the human parent raising a child and fulfilling its needs. This can, *at times*, be an effective comparison, and I will reference it when appropriate.

Researchers have discovered that the 50 most common behavioural patterns in dogs have also been witnessed in wolves. We know dogs' wolf ancestry still influences their behaviour today, such as disguising their scent with other animals' faeces, and believing it is still necessary to mark territory.

Studies are contradictory as to the exact percentage of DNA dogs have in common with wolves, but they all agree that they share at least 99.96 per cent. With this in mind, the statement that 'dogs are not wolves' can close minds to the possibility of finding valuable information to further understand dog behaviour. There are truths on each side of the debate, and it is our job, as keen dog enthusiasts, to remain open-minded. This will help us better understand the motivation behind our dogs' behaviour. A more appropriate question to explore in top-down thinking is to ask: 'how much of your dog is still part-wolf?' This leads us to the question of how much we can learn from studying wolves.

The need for a leader

The opposing theorists argue that feral dogs do not form organised packs, and so domestic dogs do not need a leader. On the surface, this reasoning would seem to make sense. However, on closer study, it appears that feral dogs have lost their way with regards to organisation. Through the evolutionary changes to their appearance, feral dogs are not physically strong or fast enough to take down large prey, and so do not get the opportunity to hone their skills and teamwork.

As a consequence of this change in the group formation, the pack is not working together as a single unit to achieve a collective goal. Instead, they act more like a group with different priorities, and so different behaviours and a different type of attachment form. Feral dogs are scavengers, and each dog will work independently for food, but being social animals, they collaborate for security and companionship. It is more akin to a bunch of friends cohabiting, where they would have some needs fulfilled together, but not all. As a result, there is often more than one breeding pair, and the father dog does not contribute as much as a wolf father, creating high pup mortality rates. So the leadership model of behaviour becomes clouded, whereas, in a functional wolf pack or human family, the co-operative group or pack of subordinates looks to their leaders to be provided with answers regarding their needs.

Observations of dysfunctional behaviour resulting in poorly-met needs and high mortality rates do not prove that a leadership model cannot exist with feral dogs, domestic dogs or people, in the same way as a *Lord of the Flies* or a poorly-run business scenario does not, either; it only proves that, through the existing circumstances, each group/pack/ tribe/family of dogs, or family of parents and young children etc., always needs clear leadership to survive and have a good quality of life.

Dogs, whatever their environment, will always have to ask fundamental questions about their survival in regards to their needs. Where is the next meal coming from? Who provides the food? Is this situation dangerous? Who is going to deal with the danger? Who is issuing the requests? Dogs need us to answer these questions by making sensible decisions regarding their needs, because they cannot effectively fulfil them for themselves. Their environment and physical appearance may have changed, but dogs have to involve humans in these questions because how effectively their owners meet their needs has a direct effect on their survival.

To disregard these questions of human influences over canines, which demonstrates either that the person will act as a caregiver or will need taking care of, denounces a dog's ability to assess others' actions regarding their needs and respond. Without this ability, the dog would not survive! Supporters of a solely bottom-up model, absent of some kind of leader, still often belie their beliefs by acting as a leader with their own dogs by providing for their needs, even if they put a different interpretation on their actions.

The evidence to support a leader/follower theory through an understanding of needs and original nature seems to be self-evident, but all observations are subject to individual interpretation. There have been countless observations of dogs that feel safe with one member of the household but not with another. I have seen many dogs change dramatically from being aggressive in trying to warn off intruders to being calm and responsive, depending on who is looking after them and whom they feel responsible for. There is a different tone to the bark used to alert another member of the family compared to that used to warn off an intruder. In the former case, the dog is looking to the human to make decisions regarding its safety, and in the latter, it has assumed responsibility for its own and others' safety. This is a clear sign of the different roles the dog fulfils in each relationship in a leader/follower scenario. It regularly comes down to the same core issue: *who thinks they are providing for whom?*

Of course, all undesirable behaviour does not mean a dog has assumed the position of leader! There are many dogs out there that simply haven't been taught the rules yet, or are just assessing what they can and cannot get away with. There is a big difference between a dog who believes it is in charge and one who needs to be taught a correct response. In both cases, the dog may need teaching the correct response, but the former type will be less open to it than the latter. Likewise, there are children who only need teaching a few times because they do not understand, and who look to their parents for guidance, whilst other children do not respect the authority of their parents, and are more likely to hold on to the control they have inadvertently been handed. In these scenarios, we also commonly refer to the children as thinking they are in charge.

Confusing terminology

Much of the confusion with and criticism of a top-down study originates from the study of wolves in an enclosed wolf park. These particular wolves had many domestic conflicts and were quite hostile toward each other, due to them being lumbered with strong personalities but unable to disperse because of being enclosed in an unnatural environment. Consider the *Big Brother* house in the TV show, where there are many different personalities cooped up together. This is a show in which we expect conflict due to the unnatural conditions. A study of unnatural, confused behaviour will lead to an unnatural, confused philosophy. The observations of the wolf park study led many to believe that if they mimicked the forceful behaviour observed in these wolves, making dogs submit to them, this would enable a person to be in charge of the dog. This, of course, doesn't make you a leader, and it is confrontational. Any study of 'language' and leadership that concentrates on how to tackle an animal instead of looking for ways to communicate with and provide for it has seriously missed the point.

So-called dominance theory has many different theories contained within it. Due to some misguided people thinking that force is the answer, all the theories in top-down thinking have been associated with force by some ever since. Force can cause serious psychological stress and harm to the dog. This has created a backlash, focusing on the differences between wolf and dog, rather than the commonalities that can aid in communication. As a result, scientists, biologists and authors with a love of animals are quick to explain that dominating your dog with force does not make you in charge – a view with which I completely agree.

Now terms such as 'dominance', 'pack leader', 'alpha', 'wolf' and even 'leader' have negative connotations for some, but what do the words actually mean?

'Alpha' means the dominant one in the pack, and dominance means having power over another – but it is not necessarily synonymous with force. Do people need power over their dogs? Yes, inasmuch as a loving parent does over a child. The parent has responsibility for the child and will make the major decisions in day-to-day life on food, security, wellbeing and confidence. The reality, despite the controversial word, is that parenting and dog ownership are benevolent dictatorships. Children and dogs do not have an equal say regarding their nurture. They can both outnumber the parents/owners and express requests like, for example, wanting to play in the park for longer. In this scenario, the parents/owners may decide to permit this or not, but it is ultimately the parents/owners who have the final word, no matter how many children/dogs are asking. If there is a relationship where the child is making the decisions and outmanoeuvring the adults, this leads to a world of confusion, as can be seen regularly on television in programmes such as *Supernanny*, in which Jo Frost comes to the parents' aid to explain how to restore a natural order in their households. The children are always happier in the end, when they are no longer running riot and the parents have become effective leaders. This scenario is the same with dogs in our home life.

As terms such as 'pack leader', 'dominance' and 'alpha' are taken out of context, I avoid using them. However, on a practical level, an individual owner's perception of what words insinuate is more important to us than it is to the dog. What is important to the dog is to have someone kind and gentle whom it can trust to fulfil its needs. Everything else is secondary.

The act of fulfilling one's needs is what I refer to in this book as 'leader'. It is clear we have to fulfil our dogs' needs and not the other way round, and no scientist, trainer or author would dispute that. Therefore, the debates about which theories are correct would benefit by shifting focus, first by seeking to understand the dogs' needs in greater depth before attempting to correct behaviour, and then to examine which normal training practices take the dogs' needs into account.

Guardian Role

The next chapters put forward a guide to help you better understand and effectively communicate to your dog with a rethink that draws information from both the top-down and bottom-up models, as well as how human parents raise children. This will be achieved by revealing:

- **Your dog's needs:** what they are and how to fulfil them.
- **Your dog's language:** how to communicate with your dog in a language it understands.
- **Your dog's emotional state:** why your dog's state becomes heightened and how to keep your dog calm.
- **An effective leadership approach:** how to become a leader your dog trusts.

Putting this study together, I refer to collectively as 'Guardian Role'.

By adopting the principles of Guardian Role, it will transform your relationship with your dog. It will enable you to both identify your dog's needs in each moment and communicate your role as the needs provider. It will empower you with the mind tools to address your dog's undesirable behaviours, whilst ensuring it is a freethinking animal that learns what you are asking from it. As a result, you will become the guardian to a happy, well-behaved dog that looks to you for guidance.

PART 2
THE METHOD

Our method to help you become the guardian of a happy and well behaved dog is achieved by understanding 4 core principles.

Chapter 3
Your Dog's Needs

"The dogs' environment, aesthetics and diet have dramatically altered but their needs will never change."
(Nigel Reed)

A hierarchy of needs

A hierarchy of needs was documented by Abraham Maslow. It is in the form of a pyramid that shows how humans are motivated to fulfil our most urgent needs, from the bottom of the pyramid first and then progressing upwards. The pyramid shows our deficiency needs, which must be fulfilled in order for us to function well. The most urgent of the deficiency needs (or deficit needs) are the physiological needs of food, water, warmth and so on, moving upwards to security, belonging and finally, esteem. Depending on our environment and culture, we will be taught different skills in order to fulfil these needs. For example, in Western society, we are taught to understand the concept of money so we can buy food; we learn how to stay safe by crossing roads, and get shelter from various forms of housing. Deep in the Amazon basin, however, so-called 'lost tribes' teach their children to hunt and live off the land, build huts and so on.

Our behaviour is tailored to fulfil our needs in the way we have learned to suit our environment. Understanding the motivation behind the actions involved in fulfilling these needs gives us a profound insight into why we act as we do. Our need for food, warmth, water, security and safety override any materialistic needs. However, as the basic needs of food, water, warmth, security and safety are normally a given to most of us in the Western world, our instincts regarding these have subsided, freeing up our time to concentrate on fulfilling higher needs. Our attempts to fulfil our 'belonging needs' can appear in many forms, including family, social groups, clubs and work. Equally, our 'esteem needs' can be fulfilled by contributing to society and feeling valued by others or ourselves.

All of us are hardwired to fulfil our needs, but we fulfil them to different extents. Without a conscious awareness of what our true needs are, and therefore how to effectively fulfil them, we could try to meet those needs in a way that is detrimental to our wellbeing. As an example of this, in many parts of the world, youths join criminal gangs to establish a sense of belonging and esteem (or in some cases, security), and then look to less-than-capable leaders for information. Being unable to effectively fulfil our own needs, or not having a leader who knows how to fulfil them for us, will create problems.

Maslow's understanding of deficit needs in human nature can be translated to canines. Fulfilling the needs of the canine is much simpler than fulfilling those of the person, as long as we learn how to do it. If we can first identify what these needs are, and then establish what actions are necessary to achieve them for the dog, this becomes the foundation of a nurturing relationship.

To keep it simple, I have removed a couple of components from Maslow's original pyramid, which stretched the definition of needs and compromised the hierarchal order. No model of behaviour is perfect, as some behaviours are innate and all are affected by the environment. The needs can overlap with one another but nevertheless, the hierarchy provides a good, simple model to help identify canine motivation and react to the most urgent needs whilst simultaneously fulfilling the others.

A wolf's needs

Simplified Maslow pyramid showing canines' deficit needs

Leader wolves are motivated to set up their territories where there are good den sites that provide water, food, resources and cover, and are away from danger. A wolf mother will look after her pups' physiological needs by feeding them her milk, cuddling them to keep them warm, and finding an appropriate den and guarding it to keep them safe. She will also keep them healthy by eating their faeces.

The leader wolves will make many conscious decisions to ensure safety for themselves, and for the wellbeing of the pack. They will mark and patrol the boundaries of the territory, sending the message to neighbouring wolves that they inhabit that territory and are not to be approached. If a wolf pack cannot find food in its own territory then their physiological needs will force them to explore other wolves' territories, thus jeopardising their security needs, but physiological needs will inevitably override the need for safety.

It is through belonging to a pack that the chances of survival are greatest, as the animals are able to work together to secure their physiological and security needs. They will find their place in the pack through play, interaction and observing the more experienced members' behaviour. It is ultimately the job of the more experienced members to prepare the young for later life, but all members contribute to the pack's wellbeing.

Once a wolf has developed to a certain age (around seven months), it will be expected to contribute to the pack's survival: to aid in hunting and keeping the pack safe by alerting the leaders to any dangers. As its skills improve, its position in the pack may elevate in terms of the regard in which it is held by the rest of the pack, which will show in the way it stands and carries itself.

Different environment, same needs

By looking to nature to see the needs of the pup being met by the wolf parents, or by using examples of good human parenting, it is possible to see that we can fulfil this role as provider for our own dogs in our environment.

The natural canine environment of the wilderness has drastically changed. They now live with people in a confusing, manmade environment of roads, cars, buses, lorries, house rules, strange sounds, other dogs and children. Although their environment has changed, dogs still have the same needs, but fulfilling these needs now requires different actions. Wolf pups look to pack leaders to fulfil their needs, and dogs look to us. Once we identify these needs for ourselves, we can get a clear insight into how to fulfil them and thus, effectively nurture dogs in our world.

A dog's needs

Physiological needs

The physiological needs are the most urgent for the dog. It needs food, water, sleep and a comfortable temperature in which to live, and without these needs being met, the dog will not survive.

Food

We have a large choice of what to feed our dogs. All dogs need a healthy diet of proteins, fats, minerals and vitamins. There are many different types of food recommended by supermarkets, vets and nutritionists, including canned food, dried food and semi-moist food. There are standard, premium, organic-holistic and natural diets. These diets vary in their claims, which of course, can become confusing. Be careful what you buy: just because something is on the shelves, does not mean that it is good for your dog; there are diets that have made it onto supermarket shelves but are full of artificial colourings, preservatives and excess bulk in the form of grain. Some dogs have problems processing the nutrients from such foods, causing them to consume more food to get what their bodies need, which can lead to excess fat and can affect the internal organs.

There are passionate people on either side of the diet debate, so in order to know what your dog is eating, it is necessary to do research. Read the packaging carefully to see if there are any artificial colourings and preservatives. Read specialist books and my blog, consult nutritionists or view independent dog-food-reviewing websites in order to form your own opinion as to what is best. If you get it right, it will save you lots of trips to the vet.

Prepared foods

Prepared foods are the most popular of diets. There are many different brands of prepared food, marketed for age and breed, so if you are thinking of using a prepared food, look for one that fits your dog's criteria at that time. Manufacturers have researched what nutrients a dog needs for each time in its life, with diets containing a balance of minerals, fats, proteins and vitamins for healthy development. For example, a growing puppy requires a specific set of minerals in order to aid bone growth, whereas an ageing dog would likely benefit from other minerals to help its joints. The two main types of prepared foods are complete and complementary.

Complete foods

Complete foods, as the name suggests, are diets that contain all the nutrients, vitamins and minerals that a dog needs.

Complementary foods

Complementary foods, such as tinned meat, are not nutritionally balanced. Some tins can contain up to 75 per cent water, so complementary foods on their own would not be an appropriate diet.

Home cooking

A home-cooked diet is a tasty, healthy option for your dog if you have the time and resources to investigate what nutrients and minerals the dog needs in each meal. But it can, of course, be a lengthier process than buying specialised foods. Check out my blog for quick, healthy meals.

The natural diet

The natural diet, otherwise known as the Raw Meat and Bones or BARF (Bones And Raw Food) diet, was developed by vets trying to recreate the diet that nature provides to ensure healthy development. It is believed that dogs can extract all the nutrients and minerals they need from raw meat. Chewing bones cleans their teeth to prevent infections and disease.

Advocates of a home-cooked and natural diet claim that many processed pet foods are linked to numerous health problems.

Water

Water is essential in the dog's diet and should always be available throughout the day. Water is required to maintain body temperature, digest food, flush out toxins, absorb nutrients and regulate acid levels. It is recommended that the water is changed twice a day to keep it fresh. If the dog is on a dry diet then they may need lots of water, as there is less moisture to extract from the food.

Body temperature regulation

Dogs need to be able to regulate their temperature at around 38.6 degrees centigrade. If a dog is hot, it regulates its temperature using the respiratory system, mainly by panting. The mouth opens, the tongue hangs out, and the dog breathes in through the nose and out through the mouth, to allow the air to cool the blood in the tongue before it reaches the lungs. The cooler blood then circulates around the rest of the body.

If a dog becomes too hot, it will be more comfortable in the shade, by a window with fresh air or resting on a cold floor. If a dog is too cold because it has a thin coat then covering it up with some material or turning up the heating may be necessary to provide warmth. It is wise to cut a dog's hair when it is getting warm and to let it grow in the colder months, particularly for breeds that do not moult.

Sleep

The breed of dog, their environment and how active they are will contribute to how much they sleep. Bigger dogs tend to sleep more. Dogs spend much of their time sleeping, and it plays an important part in their overall health. Blood pressure, body temperature and heart rate all decrease with sleep, which provides much-needed respite. Activity in the house will dictate sleeping patterns, so a relaxed environment that is free from noise and disturbance is essential. To ensure your dog has sufficient sleep, the old but relevant saying, 'let sleeping dogs lie', is paramount to its wellbeing. Many dogs have accidentally bitten people in confusion when disturbed. Provide a comfortable bed somewhere that they can go to get away from noise and attention and relax when it suits them.

Toileting

Dogs are instinctively clean animals and will rather not toilet near their 'dens', so it is important to establish their living areas and their toilet areas. How much your dog needs to toilet will vary on an individual basis (for more on toilet training, see Chapter 16). Be aware of your dog's need for the toilet throughout the day. It is important to know your dog's toilet habits in order to let the dog relieve itself if necessary before trying to train it, since training an animal when it needs the toilet will create resistance.

Safety needs

The next on the triangle is safety needs. The dog has a fundamental need not just to be safe and healthy, but also to feel safe at each moment.

Perceived dangers

The physical dangers that can cause the dog harm are a relatively short list that includes traffic, rivers, the sea, sharp objects such as glass on the floor, poisonous food, and certain people and dogs that need to be avoided. There are, however, many situations that the dog, not knowing the world as we do, can perceive as a threat, and many of which it will inevitably face. Examples include visitors, postmen, cars, buses, planes, joggers, thunder/lightning, skateboarders, cyclists, loud noises, other dogs, and even its guardians leaving (the dog not knowing if they are coming back, and feeling abandoned).

If a dog perceives the situation as frightening and is stressed as a result, then their experiences will be as traumatic for them as if the dangers were real ones. If these experiences are frequent, they will live a poor quality of life, which will in turn effect their health. It is a huge priority that the dog is not just safe, but also *feels* safe in each part of its environment.

Recall work

The human environment can be dangerous for a dog, particularly if the dog does not understand human rules and boundaries. The roads are busy with traffic and the parks are full of other dogs, as well as children and families playing or having picnics. It is always vital to get your dog to listen to you when you call it or the result could be potentially dangerous for you, your dog and others. It is advisable to keep your dog on a lead until you are sure it will come back to you when called. I will go into detail on how to achieve this later in the book.

Health

Dogs can be very good at hiding pain, a trait that served them well when they were in the wild. A perceived weakness would have meant a lower place in the pack hierarchy, which would mean less food and so less chance of survival. Behavioural issues can arise from an animal being ill or suffering from pain. If behavioural problems arise very suddenly, it is best to get the dog checked out by a vet before attempting to address the problems.

A good tip is to check your dog's health by regularly looking at its teeth, mouth, eyes, ears and feet, to see if everything looks clean and in order. Teeth need to be cleaned regularly with the aid of bones or chew sticks. If the dog has bad breath, this may be down to an infection.

Grooming can provide a good opportunity to inspect your dog's whole body, checking for lumps, inflammations, cuts, infections, skin disorders, diseases and parasites, as well as maintaining your dog's coat and strengthening your mutual bond. If you see something out of the ordinary or you are in any doubt about any aspect of your dog's health, seek advice from a vet.

Dogs are susceptible to five main diseases – parvovirus, hepatitis, distemper, leptospirosis and parainfluenza (kennel cough) – which, if contracted, can be life-threatening. There is some speculation about when boosters for immunisation are required, with some believing they should be administered annually, but others opting for every few years, so it is best to consult a trusted vet.

Breed

The breed of dog you choose can be a factor in a long list of possible health conditions that can cause serious discomfort for the dog, plus regular, expensive trips to the vet. Read up about congenital problems that can occur with some breeds. It is advisable to take out pet insurance as early as possible to help with the costs of any treatment.

Belonging needs

Next up is the dog's belonging needs. This is its need to belong to a family and receive regular company, affection and play.

Company

Dogs, being social animals, thrive on company, and enjoy it when the family is together. Leaving your dog on its own for many hours a day will provoke distress. As a guide, I would recommend not leaving your dog on its own for more than four hours a day.

Attachment

As a social animal, the dog has a hardwired need for attachment. A primary purpose of attachment is to pinpoint the responsibilities and position of each member of the pack: in other words, to determine who is in ch4arge and who makes decisions for needs' fulfilment.

All types of relationship are possible through attachment. You can have a dog who looks to you as a guardian who fulfils all its needs, a friend who fulfils some of its needs, or someone they need to take care of. The type of relationship your dog thinks it has with you is a direct result of how you communicate with it. In turn, this dictates the dog's behaviour, with the dog either looking to the human for a response and following suit, or taking on the huge responsibility to fulfil its needs in a world it does not understand.

Chapter 4 goes into more detail on how to communicate your role.

Affection

Affection strengthens the bonds between owner and dog, and enables closeness. It reduces stress levels and blood pressure for both parties. It also boosts the dog's self-esteem, allowing it to feel valued.

Play

Play is an essential part of dog development, especially in puppies, as it helps them to fine-tune motor skills and develop strength. It also helps the dog to bond with its owner, enforcing pack hierarchy, and establishing pack communication and socialisation skills. It is great for mental and physical stimulation, and can be an excellent exercise in teaching good manners. It contributes to dogs' health, too, as it is a great form of exercise.

Dogs need to be mentally and physically stimulated, but they do not all have the same preferences for games or tricks. Some dogs will see the game of fetch as the best game in the world, whereas others will be less enthusiastic about it. There are many ways to interact healthily with your dog, by playing games, teaching tricks and participating in activities that stimulate the dog, such as fetch, frisbee and agility training, among many others. These all provide great opportunities to teach the dog how to play nicely, thereby contributing to the fulfilment of its belonging and esteem needs.

Esteem needs

The fulfilment of the dog's esteem needs follows from a feeling of confidence in its environment, your ability as leader, and through an understanding of how it should behave.

Confidence

All dogs want to feel happy and relaxed in their environment. The world is full of situations, both in the home and outside, in which the dog will feel uncertain, and will need teaching and nurturing by its owner in order to feel confident it is behaving appropriately. If the dog perceives the guardian as the leader and understands it should look to him or her for its physiological and security needs, it will also get its guidance from the guardian on the rules of the environment and what is and isn't appropriate. This gives the guardian the opportunity to be viewed as the one to teach the dog what is and what is not allowed.

Teaching

In order for the dog to have confidence and know what they should be doing, they need us to teach them. If a dog is not sure what to do in a given situation, and subsequently feels confused and out of its depth, then scolding it will only have the knock-on effect of lowering its confidence and self-esteem. Our world can be a confusing place for a dog, so it may require lessons on how to behave in every situation, from meeting another dog to the arrival of visitors.

Stages

Teaching your dog lessons in confidence can be done in stages. To do this, define a starting point and identify an end goal, and then progress in stages, gradually adding more information until you reach that end goal. For example, when teaching a dog to walk to heel, first teach them in the home, as this is where they feel safe, and you will have their attention without any distractions. Once they have learnt the response, you can move on to the garden, where there are a few more distractions. Once the dog has learnt the response in the garden, go to the next stage such as a quiet residential street, and keep building the information in slowly until the dog is walking to heel in a busy environment such as a park. *At each stage, the dog must have time to assess its environment with its senses, feel comfortable, and observe you in your role as guardian.* This will ensure that you do not rush your dog, going at its pace, and only moving forward if it is happy and responsive. (I go into more detail on walking to heel and the various stages of this later in the book.)

Praise/reward

Praising your dog with enthusiastic comments (such as 'good boy' or 'good girl') and rewarding it with treats will boost its self-esteem in the knowledge that it is doing something right. Be careful to administer praise and reward at the exact moment at which the dog gets it right. Treats can be slowly reduced as the dog learns the correct response until they are no longer needed.

Consequences

On the other side of the coin, a dog needs to be corrected appropriately when it gets something wrong, in order to give it direction. Each mistake the dog makes is an opportunity to teach it. The dog will make many mistakes, and the best form of controlling a dog's behaviour is to teach it self-control: to give the dog the ability to think and learn from its mistakes. If the dog is being controlled, it will not likely learn anything.

Exploring

Dogs love to explore their environment using all their senses. Going out on a walk is a great way to achieve this; it reduces stress and anxiety and contributes to their health, as well as strengthening bonds, providing it is out there with someone it trusts to make sensible decisions. Dogs need their physiological needs to be met, to feel safe in their environment and to understand their correct place in the pack, to feel truly comfortable when going out.

Needs equals behaviour

Many factors will influence an individual dog's needs in each moment: age, body shape, personality, the environment they find themselves in, how they perceive the world, and their confidence levels. What is good for one dog is not necessarily good for another, so it is vital you are aware of what action is required to meet your dog's needs. For example, dogs with shorter noses, such as bulldogs and pugs (brachycephalic skulls) etc., will commonly suffer in the heat due to their anatomy hindering their breathing; this will consequently affect their ability to cool themselves down, whereas longer-muzzled dogs will cope better. In both scenarios, you have to be aware and vigilant if your dog is comfortable when taking them out in warm weather. But in the former scenario, you have to be hyper-vigilant.

So, as the dog's guardian, it is our role to identify our dog's needs in each moment and take the necessary actions to fulfil them, i.e. to ensure their physiological needs are met through being fed, having access to water and a place to toilet, being at the right body temperature, and free to sleep when they choose to. Their security needs are met through being and feeling safe in their environment, and through being healthy. Their belonging needs are met through having regular company, interaction and play, wherein they gain an understanding of their rightful position in the family/pack. And their esteem needs are met by feeling confident, both in their environment and in the people around them, through being taught how to behave in a calm, consistent manner.

If the guardian fails to meet the dog's needs or if the dog believes it is has to fulfil its own needs then it will resist the guardian's requests and/or step up and fulfil the leader role. The dog's attempts to fulfil the job will manifest in a range of undesirable behaviours, including issues with food, barking at visitors, aggression towards other dogs or towards people, nervousness, not listening to/challenging the guardian, attempting to manoeuvre family members (invading personal space, jumping up, nudging, barking/whining to get attention), persistent following, separation anxiety, pulling on the lead, freezing on the walk, obsessive behaviour, toileting in the house, and much more. The fact that the dog is not qualified to do the job because it does not understand the world does not come into its thinking, as someone has to do it.

Think inside the triangle

Problem behaviour may derive from just one unmet need, a couple, a few, or all. So it will not always be obvious which needs are being flagged up by any particular behaviour, especially as dogs cannot talk to us in any human language. For example, a dog that is losing too much weight obviously needs to eat more food, but if plenty of food is readily available to them and they are leaving it uneaten, then this behaviour could be a result of stress, induced by confusion of roles.

A dog chewing in the home may be down to a physiological need because they are teething, a security need (they are chewing because they feel anxious), a belonging need (they are unhappy at being left alone for too many hours a day), or a lack of confidence (the guardian may simply have not told them what they *can* chew), and many other concerns related to any combination of their unmet needs.

Likewise, a dog pulling (or freezing) on the lead may be motivated to do so by a physiological need, such as having to go to the toilet, looking for food, or avoiding uncomfortable weather conditions, or a security need, such as feeling unsafe, resulting in the dog pulling forward or backwards, whilst appearing uncomfortable and unresponsive. It could also be due to confusion around their belonging needs, believing they should be making the decisions about where to go and at what speed, or a lack of confidence, from simply not being taught the correct response – or any combination of these issues.

Misidentifying the dog's need behind the behaviour will cause the guardian to address it with an incorrect action, leaving the actual need unmet. For example, if a guardian takes the dog out and it pulls on the lead, the guardian may think this is due to a lack of confidence (i.e. they just need teaching how to walk to heel), but it could be down to the dog's perceived security needs. If this is the case then if the dog tries to flee when confronted with a situation it perceives as a danger, the guardian may wrongly correct them when they pull, instead of demonstrating that they understand their concerns and will protect them. This will cause the dog to resist the guardian's action, making the lesson unnecessarily difficult and traumatic for the dog.

Also, if a dog displays aggressive behaviour and the guardian assumes it is because of a confusion in their belonging needs and them feeling responsible for the pack's safety, but it is actually due to the dog being in significant pain (physiological/security need), then they will not receive the medical care they desperately need. However, if the guardian identifies the dog's need, they can assess the environment and proceed with a correct course of action.

To identify the motivation behind the dog's problem behaviour, start with the most urgent needs – physiological – and work up from there. So if you are taking your dog out for a walk and it starts pulling or freezing on the lead, and you want to teach them to walk to heel, consider their physiological needs first – making sure they are not hungry or thirsty, the weather conditions are right (it is not too hot, cold or wet), they do not desperately need the toilet and are not tired – as well as other needs, such as that they feel safe and are in good health. Be patient and clear in communicating your role, whilst teaching the desired response in stages so they understand the message and you do not rush their learning. *Whatever the issue, consider the possibility of the undesirable behaviour stemming from any combination of unmet needs.*

The canine paradox

One of the primary reasons so many guardians fail to identify a dog's unmet needs behind problem behaviour is due to the widely-used model that we use today to address the dog's nurture. This model consists of a list of six areas that comprise of some of the dog's needs, and actions to fulfil those needs: food, socialisation, exercise, health, training, and ensuring a relaxed environment. To some extent, this list resembles the needs in the pyramid. Food is a physiological need. Socialisation is designed to boost the dog's confidence needs with other dogs. Exercise and health contribute to security needs. Training is designed to create positive behaviours, and a relaxed environment contributes to their physiological needs of sleep and health. However, as this list does not include *all* the dog's needs, or a priority order for them to be fulfilled, *it can result in many guardians following the list with tunnel vision, whilst unknowingly neglecting their dog's other needs.*

For example, I often hear guardians claim, 'My dog does not like going out when it is raining', to which I would reply, 'Then do not take your dog out for a walk when it is raining'. People often look puzzled by this response, due to the deep-set belief that you must strictly abide by the list and take your dog out a certain number of times a day, rain or shine, or you are a bad dog owner. Simply put, if the dog does not want to go out and is communicating a physiological preference to stay dry, warm or out of the heat, then it is not necessary to take them out.

Guardians may comment that their dog will misbehave in the home if they do not walk them for a certain amount of time per day. The dog not having enough exercise is often used as an excuse for undesirable behaviour. But undesirable behaviour frequently originates from a different unmet need altogether. For example, the dog could be pacing up and down in the home and garden in an attempt to deal with perceived security needs. Or it could be on its feet all day, pestering the guardian because it believes it is the leader and so decides when to interact. This misunderstanding of taking the dog out for exercise, especially into an environment where it fears for its safety, will likely produce further problematic behaviours outside, such as the dog barking at other dogs to deal with its perceived security needs, or pulling on the lead and/or being unresponsive off lead, because it believes it is making the decisions on the walk.

The undesirable behaviour that occurred in the home may in some cases appear to be reduced after a walk, as the dog has burnt off its nervous energy. An observation of calmer behaviour then may falsely reaffirm to the guardian that exercise is what the dog needed. However, walking the dog for these reasons fails to identify or address why the problematic behaviour occurred in the first place. Exercising the dog in this scenario is another case of treating the symptoms rather than the disease. As a result, the dog will wake up the next day with the same problem behaviours and the guardian will likely repeat the same exercising and distraction technique. All that is really achieved by doing this is producing a fitter dog. Likewise, if you had debts and decided to go for a run, you will likely feel better afterwards. However, the next day, you would wake up with the same problems.

Take another example from the list: socialising your dog. Socialising is designed to boost the dog's confidence needs by getting them used to other dogs. This is usually a successful exercise because it is done when the dog is a puppy, and so typically, has not assumed the leader role. The majority of dogs (if socialised with well-behaved dogs) learn for themselves that other dogs are not a threat. As some of these dogs get older and stronger, they assume the leader role. They can then become so overwhelmed with the responsibilities that they become aggressive towards or fearful of other dogs, despite already being socialised. People then observe the problematic behaviour and assume the dog has not been socialised, even though it has.

This is not to say exercise or socialising is not important – both are. It's just that, when partaking in any activity with the dog, *it is vital all of their needs are being fulfilled in the process, whilst communicating that you are providing for their needs.*

When guardians experience problem behaviour with their dogs, they will look for a solution in the form of training. However, if the training technique controls or distracts the dog rather than building up its confidence, whilst communicating that the guardian will provide for it in all areas, then it will likely meet resistance. If the technique is successful in stopping the behaviour, the dog may learn helplessness in that situation and suffer in silence.

All around the world, guardians have been brainwashed to train, socialise and exercise their dogs, yet so many cases of problem behaviour exist because guardians miss the most fundamental issue to the dogs' wellbeing: the dogs' needs and what actions are necessary to meet them. The moment we shift into autopilot, addressing this generic list of actions to address our dogs' nurture rather than looking at their needs as a whole and assessing what they need at each point in time, is the moment we inadvertently discard our most basic nurturing instincts. Replacing the list with the hierarchical model and considering all needs in every event will result in a more effective, mindful approach. In turn, this will allow a two-way communication to take place, which will strengthen your relationship with your dog with the knowledge that you understand its concerns.

Chapter 4
Your Dog's Language

"The dog cannot fully comprehend our language but we can learn theirs." (Jan Fennell)

Dogs are oblivious to knighthoods, medals, qualifications, money or positions at work. The self-appointed title of owner, parent or guardian does not convince a dog – nor a child, for that matter – of leadership. What does convince the dog is a leader who is active, capable and trusted to fulfil its needs.

We know that we are the best ones to make the major decisions regarding the dog's needs, as we understand the human environment. We know safety from danger, we provide the food and we decide where to go. So why is it that some dogs do not understand this?

Communication issues

People's communication varies with dogs, depending on how they look. As a result, different dogs will get different information about their environment and the corresponding rules. Generally, smaller dogs' actions are interpreted and responded to differently from those of larger breeds. For example, if a Jack Russell jumps up at a person, it is often rewarded with a stroke or a gentle greeting. On the other hand, if a Great Dane jumps up at someone, it is seen as badly behaved and intrusive. This is less likely to be tolerated, so will be treated completely differently. The small dog is perceived as sweet and the large as having bad manners. As a result, the behaviour of the smaller dog is often deemed acceptable and is ignored, whilst the larger animal is considered a problem that needs to be dealt with.

Lap dogs that bite anyone who approaches them can have their aggressive behaviour casually attributed to the 'snappy nature' of the breed, but in reality, such problems often arise due to human behaviour toward them. Many people's hearts melt when they see them and they want to stroke them. But the dog, not understanding the person's kind intentions, will be more concerned that its space is being intruded upon. The initial response is looking uncomfortable or growling. If these responses haven't worked previously and people persist in invading its space, the dog will learn a new response: to fight (bite). In this instance, the person will pull away and the dog thinks it has been successful because the person has backed off. Over time, a learned pattern of behaviour solidifies in the dog's mind that aggression works, much to the dismay of many well-intentioned humans. Yet, if a larger dog looks uncomfortable and growls, it is much more likely to be listened to.

I can recall, when teaching a Rottweiler to heel, that people would not approach me, especially in winter, when I was wearing a hooded jacket. Conversely, when I was teaching a French Bulldog to walk to heel, many people approached to pet him, unwittingly giving him confusing signals and disturbing the teaching process. This particular French Bulldog had aggression problems. This was most likely due to strangers ten times his size approaching him and sticking their hands in his face, thinking he was cute and ignoring the universal rule of personal space. The dog had no idea of the person's kind intentions but instead, saw people invading his space. In this case, as in many others, good looks and cuteness can be a curse.

We may encourage bad behaviour by not thinking consciously about what our communication means to the dog, when they are puppies, for instance, because it looks cute and amusing when they are running about frantically barking. However, when such a dog is fully grown, jumping up on the sofa and barking around the house, it paints a very different picture.

Whilst interacting with dogs, we are in communication with them, and therefore, our actions carry meaning. All dogs have communication patterns and movements that they evaluate, no matter what age, size or breed they are. If we want to maintain a successful relationship with our dogs, we need to understand their communication methods and, most importantly, use them to get our message across. Dogs are not able to learn our often inconsistent language, but we have the ability to adapt and learn theirs.

Body language, tonality and words

Professor Albert Mehrabian, a communication expert, orchestrated studies into human communication and discovered that our language is made up of 55 per cent body language (posture, facial expression, etc.), 38 per cent tonality (how we use our voices), and 7 per cent words (what we actually say). At first glance, the percentage for words seems absurd, as talking is such a big part of our daily communication. But if you think about it, our senses pick up all sorts of messages from non-verbal language. We notice mood changes and potential problems with people in less than a second. We can detect inconsistencies in facial or body expressions when people are lying or are being insincere. This is not to say that words are not important, as they are still vital for understanding intentions; it is just that we are so used to being on autopilot with our body language and tonality that we do not give it much conscious thought.

This statistic begs two questions. Firstly, what percentages of body language, tonality and words does the dog look for when communicating with people? Secondly, how can we utilise our language to reassure the dog that we are their leader?

In the evolution from wolf to dog, we know that the dog developed an understanding of some human language (studies show dogs look to us to solve problems where wolves do not), so there will be more comprehension of words and tonality than their predecessors. It is also clear that the dog's comprehension of human communication will be based more on our body language, due to them not being able to communicate as we do. Taking this into account, we know that the body language percentage would be way more than 55 per cent. I would postulate that body language would make up at least 90 per cent of the language that dogs interpret, leaving tonality and words at 10 per cent, at the most.

Whatever the exact statistic, it is clear that our body language is the most important factor to demonstrate that we will provide for the dog's needs, and our tonality and words must work alongside it to ensure our messages are clear. This fact is often overlooked, and it is the main reason for a breakdown in communication between owners and their dogs.

Miscommunication

> *"The single biggest problem in communication is the illusion it has taken place."* (George Bernard Shaw)

If we examine how the largest parts of our language (body and tonality) look from the dog's perspective, it becomes clear why the question of who holds the role of guardian becomes confused. Common examples of this are when the dog perceives danger.

When someone comes to the home and posts a leaflet through the letterbox, the dog, not knowing the delivery person's intentions, alerts the pack to the perceived danger by barking. However, we know the delivery person's intentions, so often, we try to quieten the dog in frustration. The dog assesses our body language and tonality at such times and sees a lack of positive action because, as far as it is concerned, we are failing to check out the danger. It therefore can perceive our attempt to silence it as us looking to it to protect us. In its mind, we are putting it in the role as leader. The harsh tone from the guardian to quieten it only reinforces its assumption that it is its responsibility to protect the pack. If the dog doesn't see the guardian taking care of what it perceives as danger in a convincing, physical manner, it will try to fill the vacuum.

In such instances, we may see 'success' in the form of the dog quietening down because we are controlling or distracting them, but this does little for the dog's confidence in your ability to take care of its safety needs, and so is often just a temporary fix.

This type of non-verbal communication would carry huge meaning in our language. Imagine a scenario in which a heart surgeon, performing major surgery, looks at the nurses every five seconds – the nurses are more than likely to ask if the doctor is okay, as the constant glances demonstrate uncertainty rather than a convincing capability. Now add a frustrated tone to the doctor's voice and imagine what the nurses would think. Even if the doctor said everything was okay, the nurses would not be convinced because of the overriding message given by the doctor's body language and tonality. If the doctor was seen to be doing everything in order and did not look up then the team would assume everything was fine.

I recall witnessing an owner struggling to communicate with her dogs whilst out with a young client called Tanal and his boxer dog Bentley. We were teaching Bentley to walk to heel on a quiet road when we saw a lady walking five Pekinese dogs. The dogs were alarmed by our presence and started barking. The lady was clearly frustrated and so started to shush them. Her verbal commands were clear to us, as we have a good understanding of human communication and what she wanted – for her dogs to be quiet. But from the dogs' point of view, they were meaningless. The dogs would look at her body language, see that she was standing behind them and appeared agitated, frustrated and aggressive, and simply think she was joining in with the barking to keep us away!

A dog starts barking or patrolling because it is actively fulfilling its perceived need to keep the pack safe. And of course, it appears to work; the leaflet delivery person would have left shortly after the dog barked, and Tanal and I did not go any closer to the five Pekinese dogs. As a result, the dogs have learned an effective but incorrect response, as well as an abdication of responsibility on behalf of the owner. On the other hand, if a dog sees the guardian addressing any problems by using convincing body language and a calm tone each time they appear concerned, no matter how trivial it appears to us, the dog will assess our language, see that we acknowledge it and are doing something, and see us as the leader.

Actions aligned with intentions

There are many other scenarios in our daily life where dogs do not understand the guardian's role as needs provider, due to an absence of language and conscious thought. In the case of a guardian letting a dog pull on the lead, the guardian could perceive this as harmless, especially if they were a small breed. But the dog could interpret the guardian's lack of correction as not fulfilling the role as leader because they are out in front, dictating the speed of the walk. Of course, you know you are making the decisions about where to go and at what speed, but does a dog pulling in front know that for sure, especially if you go on the same walk each day? If a child were walking in front of their parent and not listening, the parent would instantly address the issue because there is an underlying safety issue and they need the child to be aware of who is making the decisions. The child is not necessarily making a conscious decision to lead, but each time the parent corrects this, they reinforce the natural order of the grown-up being the decision-maker.

What message does a dog receive regarding its physiological needs and its guardian's role as food provider if food is available to them all day? Again, *you* know you are the provider, but the message can be confusing to the dog if they have access to food as and when they please. If there is any room at all for a dog to misinterpret their role then many will. If your dog is free to jump on you whenever they wish and can get your attention, but refuses to come when called, what does that say about who the decision-maker is from the dog's perspective? We know we are the needs provider and decision-maker, but if our language does not demonstrate this convincingly, it will cause the dog to question our leadership.

In the wild, wolves all speak the same language and so the hierarchical order is clear. The next section reveals the language that the leaders in the wolf pack use to demonstrate that they are the decision-makers, and so are providing for the subordinates' needs.

Canine leadership language

"Leadership is practiced, not so much in words as in attitude and in actions." (Harold S. Geneen)

Wolf behaviour is complex and changes according to their individual needs in each moment and environment. However, general principles of wild wolf behaviour have taught us that leaders demonstrate their position in four key areas.

The four points

1. Food: It is the leaders' job to find food. Once the food is caught, it is the leaders who have power over the food, and they often take advantage of this by eating first. Once they have finished, they give the signal to the subordinates that it is their turn next by walking away from the food.

2. Perceived danger: If danger approaches the pack, be it in the form of other wolves, humans or bears, etc., it is the job of all wolves to alert the rest of the pack, but it is the leaders who step up and decide what to do about it. If the leaders check out the perceived problem and are seen to be fine with whatever it is, they will not react and neither will the pack, as they trust the leaders' decisions. However, if the leaders

are troubled by the danger, they have an inbuilt defence response to deal with it. They are the 3 Fs:

Flight (running away)

Freeze (standing their ground and barking)

Fight

They are in that order for a good reason: flight is the first response, as it does them the least harm. There are, however, situations in which a wolf can't run away because they are boxed in, so they have to use the next response – freeze. Their hackles rise and they stand their ground while barking or growling. If this response has not worked and the threat keeps on coming closer then they will have one last option – fight.

3. Status: There are certain rules and elements of language that are synonymous with status. For example, when the leaders reunite with the rest of the pack after each separation, they will communicate their status. This is necessary as the pack formation could change during separation due to injury, so it is vital they assess and decipher who is in charge in these moments. The leaders communicate their status to the rest of the pack when reuniting by withholding from communicating. This sends a powerful and clear message that says: 'I'm in charge; I haven't invited you to interact with me.' If the subordinates do approach whilst the leaders display these signals, they risk getting told off. When it is time to interact, it is the leaders that make the first move by looking at the subordinates. In this moment, it is the job of the subordinates to go up to the leaders, rather than the other way round. Once invited, the subordinates never invade the leaders' space or try to make

themselves appear bigger than the leaders, whose personal space is respected at all times. This rule of the leaders deciding when it is time to interact, or to play, carries throughout the day.

4. On the hunt: The leaders in the wolf pack lead the hunt. They decide when to go, where to go and at what speed. They set the pace, direction and time to hunt, and the others follow.

Despite the lengthy evolutionary process and change in environment, canines still have the same deficiency needs and process the same internal questions about other pack members around them.

- Food – who has the right to priority feeding (a physiological need and esteem need that facilitates attachment)?
- Perceived danger – whose job is it to deal with danger (a safety and esteem need that facilitates attachment)?
- Status – who is in charge, who instigates attention after separations and throughout the day, and who instigates play (an esteem need that facilitates attachment)?
- The hunt – who leads the hunt, or in the present day, who leads the walk (a safety and esteem need that facilitates attachment)?

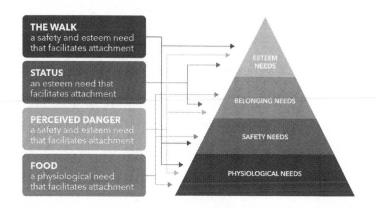

The leaders in the wild answer these questions with language, and are seen to be fulfilling their role. The subordinate wolves learn many lessons through observation, allowing them to understand their place in the pack.

If we adopt the language that leader wolves use in the wild and translate it to our home life, this will physically demonstrate to our dogs, in a language they understand, that we take charge in the four main areas that relate to their needs.

The language that follows makes no assumptions about us being in charge, but instead allows the dog to see us being effective in the leadership role by using body language, tonality and words to match the message, so our dog sees us take clear ownership of each need.

Becoming a leader

1. Food

In the wild, it is the job of the leaders to find food, and they have priority feeding.

81

Canine question: who is responsible for feeding the pack, and who gets priority to eat first?

Answer: the guardian.

gesture eating (when bowl is deserted, pick it up).

Your aim: to show your dog that you are the food provider; it is you who is entitled to priority feeding, and then you feed your dog without any fuss.

To reinforce the message to our dogs that we are the food providers and have priority feeding, we mimic the leaders' behaviour from the wild with a practice known as 'gesture eating'. To do this, after you have prepared your dog's food, put the bowl close to you but out of your dog's reach, somewhere like a kitchen counter, and then eat something, like a biscuit, piece of fruit or chocolate, so your dog sees you eating first. Once you have finished, put the bowl down by your feet and walk away. This demonstrates that you are the food provider and that you get priority feeding, and walking away is the signal that it is your dog's turn to eat. Make sure your dog is left to eat in peace without anyone approaching it.

Once your dog has eaten, it will walk away from the bowl. It is then vital to pick the bowl up, whether it is full, half-full or empty. The reason for this is that if your dog leaves some food and can come back and pick at it throughout the day, the message becomes compromised. We want to make it as clear as possible, with no room for error; picking up the bowl after your dog has left will teach the dog that it does not have access to food as and when it pleases.

When gesture eating, you should not make eye contact with or speak to your dog (including telling them to sit or wait), as the message needs to be simple; you are letting your dog learn by observing your actions. Also, do not feed your dog if it starts barking or pestering you, in an attempt to tell you when it is feeding time. Do not forget: you decide when it is time to eat. If this happens, ignore your dog until it settles down and, when you decide to, begin the feeding process.

2. Perceived danger

In the wild, it is the leaders' job to deal with perceived danger. Wolves have an inbuilt defence response to deal with danger, the three Fs:

Flight (run away)
Freeze (stand their ground, change their posture, bark, growl)
Fight

To work with the dog's nature and communicate that we provide for them, we must acknowledge their concerns regarding perceived danger to demonstrate that we understand it is there and are okay with it. If they still appear concerned, we must adopt one of the defence responses of flight or freeze. This will show them that we are defending them. *The environment and situation will dictate which defence response can be used.*

Canine question: when perceived danger approaches, who is going to protect the pack?
Answer: the guardian.

<u>inside the home</u>: by thanking, looking and, if necessary, isolating.

<u>outside the home</u>: by thanking and, if necessary, reacting (flight or freeze).

Your aim: to demonstrate to your dog that you take care of all dangers inside and outside the house. Once they alert you to a danger, you acknowledge the problem and they will instantly be at ease.

Inside the home

In the home, when visitors approach, the dog has nowhere to flee, so it will often choose the second defence response – to freeze – which can manifest itself in the form of barking. In a moment when danger presents itself, you need to display a calm reaction to show your dog you are aware of the danger.

So, for example, if the doorbell rings, causing your dog to bark, you should thank your dog for doing its job by saying 'good boy/girl' or 'thank you' in a happy tone. After all, it is a subordinate's job to alert the leader. If your dog continues to bark, you should go to have a look at what the problem is, demonstrating the clear message that you acknowledge their concerns and are investigating the situation. By this time, many dogs will observe your calm reaction to the perceived danger and, seeing that you are okay with it, will calm down. If, however, you have investigated the perceived danger and your dog is still barking and behaving erratically then you need to isolate it. You can do this by gently taking hold of its collar and putting it in another room and closing the door. You should not speak to or look at your dog at any point during this action, as doing so will confuse the message. By isolating your dog, you are giving it time to calm down and reflect on what happened, whilst also conveying the powerful signal that you are the one who deals with danger and that being stressed results in them being separated from the pack.

Once your dog has calmed down and stopped barking, you can let it join you again. Do not look at your dog when you let it rejoin the pack; rather, just go back to what you are doing. To reinforce the message that it is not its job to worry, you should also tell visitors/family members not to look at or speak to your dog when it returns to the room, as this can be perceived as looking to them for action. If your dog continues to bark, repeat the process until it relaxes and understands that you are dealing with things.

Reassuring signals that you are the leader

Saying thank you when your dog barks shows it that the role of alerting you to potential dangers to the pack is vital. By getting up and looking at the problem, you are showing it that you are dealing with the issue, and by isolating your dog, you are demonstrating that erratic behaviour will result in separation from the pack. When using this method, remember to do it quickly and calmly.

Outside

If your dog appears concerned by any danger outside, we must acknowledge that we are aware of and okay with the situation by saying 'thank you' or 'it's okay' in a happy tone. If the foundations are strong in the home, this may be enough for your dog to calm instantly. If it still looks alarmed then we must react before it does by using the safest defence response: flight, or walking off in the opposite direction. This will show it that we have acknowledged the problem and are doing something about it. If flight is not an option, because there are dogs coming from either side of you, or if the dog is only mildly concerned, then the next option is to freeze, which can be done by taking your dog by the collar and putting it behind you. Once it relaxes, you can release your grip. This will show your dog we are listening and reacting to its concerns, and in turn, it will learn to trust our decisions. I go into this in greater detail in Chapter 8.

It does not matter where the perceived danger comes from, be it in the garden or at the window, dogs on the television or in the park, thunder and lightning or just letters coming through the door. Your dog will need your acknowledgement and calm reaction to understand that you are dealing with the problem.

3. Status

In the wild, the leaders reinforce their status by deciding when it is time to interact. This is reinforced when reuniting after separations and throughout the day. The leader wolves do not approach the subordinates; rather, the subordinates are invited into the leaders' space.

Canine questions: the pack had split and has now reunited – who is in charge? Who decides when it is time to interact/play and whose job is it to go up to whom?

Answers: the guardian.
by going through the 'golden five-minute' ritual after every separation – followed by interaction through invitation only (instigating attention and play). You do

not go up to your dog; your dog must come to you.

Your aim: for your dog to be happy on your return, but remain calm and respectful of your (and any visitor's) personal space, staying back until invited in all situations, including after separations and throughout the day.

To make this message of status clear to your dog, we use the technique called the 'golden five minutes'. Every time there is a separation from your dog, no matter how long or how short (you could have come back from the bathroom or from a holiday), the pack has to reunite and the hierarchy has to be determined again. To maintain your status as decision-maker, withhold from greeting your dog until it calms down and leaves you alone – and by holding back the greeting, I mean do not touch, look at or speak to your dog. We call this the golden five minutes because silence is golden and five minutes is the average amount of time it takes when you start this process for a dog to calm down and leave you alone. Some dogs are more tenacious than others and will carry on with inappropriate behaviour, so if that's the case, just keep withholding your greeting until they learn the right response, which is to leave you alone and respect your space until you call them.

During this period, your dog may question your leadership by trying to get your attention with all sorts of behaviour, such as staring and barking at you, entering your personal space, nudging you, leaning on you, jumping up at you, pawing you, resting its chin on you, following you, getting on top of the couch, bringing you toys or cushions, and many other behaviours to get you to acknowledge its presence. It is so important during this period not to look at or speak to the dog. If you tell it to get down, it has still manipulated you into acknowledging it.

Remember, the leader cannot be manipulated or outmanoeuvred; everything that happens is on your terms. If the dog's behaviour becomes intrusive then there will have to be a consequence to this action. The initial consequence would be to push your dog away without looking at or speaking to it, firmly but with no anger. This is a gentle reminder to let your dog know to wait until invited. If you have done that a couple of times and the dog persists with intrusive behaviour then gently take the dog by the collar and isolate it in another room where it cannot see you, giving it time to reflect on what just happened. Once the dog is calm, you can let it out, but still maintain withholding the greeting. If their behaviour persists, repeat the process until it leaves you alone.

Once the dog has left you alone then you can look at them and call them into your space and instigate the attention. You can then cuddle, play, make a fuss, whatever you want. It does not matter, as long as it is on your terms.

This should carry on throughout the day, be it in the form of affection or play. So if your dog is trying to instigate attention from you, withhold the interaction until they leave you alone and it happens on your terms. *Also, do not go up to your dog; always call them to you.* This will ensure a clear, natural order of who instructs whom.

Do not think of yourself as rude when doing this. Instead, think of yourself as a decision-maker, teaching the dog manners about personal space in a language it understands. You may separate from your dog many times a day, so the process needs to be repeated each time you reunite.

4. The walk

In the wild, it is the leaders that lead the hunt. They decide where they go, when and at what speed. The closest thing the domestic dog has to a hunt is a walk.

Canine question:	who leads the walk, when and where do we go, and at what pace?
Answer:	the guardian.
	<u>on the lead</u>: by stopping, starting and changing direction. Identify stages and practice manoeuvres.
	<u>off the lead</u>: by calling once and then leaving.
Your aim:	to go out for a walk with the dog at heel on a loose leash by your side, with you deciding the direction, pace and distance of each walk. Once you let the dog off the lead, they look to see where you are, respond to your requests and follow you, no matter what distractions are around.

To ensure the dog feels safe and is not distracted, start the lesson in the home where distractions are at a minimum. This is a great place to teach a dog because it should feel safe and relaxed and can therefore concentrate on the task in hand.

To teach your dog to walk nicely to heel, first practise walking around the home without the lead, but with praise and food rewards to encourage the dog to stay by your side, rewarding it on a regular basis when it gets it right. This will get the dog into the habit of listening to you and watching where you are going. If it follows you off the lead in the home, it is doing so of its own free will, giving it a feeling of comfort and you an opportunity to teach it patiently. If you cannot get the dog's co-operation, it means it is not ready to listen. If that is the case, abandon the lesson and try again later. When the dog does decide to participate, which usually happens fairly quickly, as it understands that being next to you receiving praise and rewards is a good place to be, you are ready to begin the first stage of the walk.

As your dog improves, you can slowly progress through the stages, each one containing more distractions. If you skip stages, missing the necessary foundations for the dog's development, it can create problems down the line, as it is not yet ready to move on. So remember, there is no hurry. Take your time and be happy and in control at each stage.

On lead

The first stage is to pick up the lead and call the dog to you to put the lead on. The dog may become overexcited at the sight of the lead and jump up, run around, nudge you or make too much noise. If it does react in such an undesirable manner or is in any heightened state then put the lead back down again. This will demonstrate to the dog that you do not move forward until it gets it right. Repeat the lesson of picking the lead up and putting it back down again until it reacts in a calm manner and comes over to you. Resist asking the dog to sit and stay whilst you are doing this as it will not be learning anything; in fact, you will be removing the dog's capacity to think and work out for itself what it should be doing.

Once the dog is in a calm state, you are ready to put the lead on and move to the next stage. If the dog does not come to you then do not go out for a walk; the dog is either clearly testing you or not giving you permission to move forward. If you then approach it, put the lead on and take it out, whether due to a lack of time or for any other reason, it will create more resistance later on. If this is the case, again, abandon the lesson and try again later until you get the desired response.

Once you have the lead on and the dog is calm and relaxed, the second stage is to walk around the house, once again, encouraging it to your side with food rewards and praise. If the dog gets it wrong by pulling forward, correct the mistake using a method called stop/start/change direction. This involves stopping every time the dog drifts in front of you and pulls on the lead, moving back a few metres and encouraging it back to your chosen side. Once the dog is in the desired position (facing the direction in which you are going and the lead is loose), wait a few seconds so that it can process the information about what has just happened, and then start again (or change your direction altogether).

If the dog is getting it right by following you, reward it with a treat or praise it. Once the dog gets it, you can further reduce your feedback to build up the time before you reward or praise it. Make sure to only reward your dog whilst it is in the correct position, looking forward and walking on your desired side. By reaching over to the dog's side with a food treat in the direction of its mouth, your body language and the reward are enough to indicate that the dog is in the correct position.

At first, you can look at your dog to encourage it, but it is necessary to build up to looking where you are going. This can be achieved by looking forward for a short moment whilst praising the dog before looking at it again. As the dog gets used to these short moments with you looking forward, build up the time until the dog understands that being beside you whilst you look ahead is the correct thing to do. You need to be looking forward, not only to avoid obstacles, but also to reinforce to the dog that you are making decisions as to where you are going. If the dog gets it wrong, gently put it back in the right position and start again; it will learn where it is supposed to be.

Make sure to only reward your dog **whilst it is in the correct position**, looking forward and walking on your desired side.

Looking forward is saying, 'This is where we are going.' Looking at the dog is asking, 'Where are we going?'

Repeating this method in the house lays the foundations for a good walk. Keep practising and get it perfect in the home. If a dog does not listen to you in the home, with no distractions, then it will definitely not listen to you outside with all the sights, smells and other distractions you'll come across.

Practice manoeuvres

Whilst still in the home, make sure your dog gets its cues from you, listening to and watching you, by making your movements unpredictable. Turn, speed up, slow down or stop, praising or rewarding each time the dog listens to you. If it gets it wrong go back and practise again until it is in sync with your actions. When making a manoeuvre, make a soft noise, like a clicking or kissing noise, and show the dog a food reward as it follows, rewarding it with praise. When you have done this a number of times, you will see that the noise conditions the response and you will not even need to show the dog the food, although you can reward it afterwards whilst it is still learning. Eventually, just the movement will be enough and the rewards will not be necessary.

Encourage the dog to look at the speed at which you go. Once the dog learns to slow down when you are slowing, teach it to stop. You can practise this by slowing down gradually until you stop, and if the dog is still behind you, reward it. If the dog has drifted in front of you, gently get it back behind your feet and keep practising the manoeuvre until it gets it right.

Once you and your dog have mastered these skills, the third stage is to practise the same manoeuvres walking around the garden. If you do not have a garden then go on to the next stage.

Now you can walk around the house and garden, and you feel the dog is stopping, turning, speeding up and slowing down when you are, the fourth stage is to walk out the front door. If, when you open the door, the dog rushes out, then gently pull it back in and close the door. Once the dog is calm, open the door again. Keep repeating until the dog is relaxed and waits for you to walk through first. If it rushes out a hundred times, you pull it back in and shut the door a hundred times. Once again, do this without talking; let the dog work out what it should be doing from the consequences of its actions.

The fifth stage, after you have successfully practised the previous manoeuvres, is to continue from your front door and look for a quiet area such as a residential street in which to build upon the techniques. Keep correcting the dog by stopping and coming back a few metres, starting and moving again/changing direction (SSCD). Keep away from other distractions by leading the dog in a different direction, again, showing it that you decide where to go.

Once the dog stays to heel and follows you away from distractions, you can move on to stage six, further afield to a busier place such as a street with more activity with cars, people and other distractions. Walk up and down the street, all the time encouraging your dog to stay by your side, practising the manoeuvres. If you or the dog feel anxious then go back to a stage at which you both felt comfortable and progress from there.

As your dog becomes comfortable by your side, pick an even busier location, with many distractions. Further stages should gradually increase in difficulty due to the number of distractions, but make sure that you are both comfortable with each stage before advancing. The stages will vary according your environment, so plan ahead and seek appropriate spaces for each stage, starting off in a quiet place and building gradually.

The next stage could be a park, full of other dogs and children. Again, if your dog pulls as soon as it gets there then turn around, walk back and try again. Keep repeating until you can successfully walk through the park with the dog on the lead.

Off lead

Once the dog is walking to heel and you want to let it have a play, it is vital to know that it will come back when called, so the next levels of development involve practising recall. First, practise the recall response in the home. Begin by looking at your dog and calling it to you, using its name and saying 'come' in an enthusiastic voice. If your dog does not come to you, do not go to it or start repeating yourself; just try again later. If it does come to you, reward it with a treat, and/or praise it with a comment such as 'good girl/boy'. Once the dog correctly responds to your request in the home, you can progress to the garden and keep practising recall there.

Once your dog responds correctly each time you call it in the garden and home, the next stage could be practising in an enclosed area. This will allow you to see if your dog is listening to you outside without putting it in any danger.

Call the dog once, and if it does not come back to you, immediately walk in the opposite direction. This sends the message that you are making the decisions about where to go on the walk and you are not going to be drawn into a conversation; the dog will likely assess this information and follow you. In the unlikely event that it does not follow, it is necessary to keep practising until you get the desired response before moving on to somewhere else.

The following chapters go into more detail on this:

Chapter 12 – teaching your dog to walk to heel.

Chapter 13 – teaching your dog to come when called.

Summary

All four points need to be addressed together and consistently. It can be tempting to relax in one area if it does not cause you too much grief, but the dog will not be happy having any responsibility, and as soon as it has it in one area, it is likely to push and question in others. You have to address all the behaviour as a whole.

Using the above 'language' demonstrates that you are the leader and will fulfil the dog's needs. This gives you the platform to teach your dog and boost its self-esteem. As a result, the dog will trust your judgements and decisions and follow your lead.

As the decision-maker, you will become:

1. **Leader around food** – your dog understands that you will provide the food and are entitled to priority feeding.

2. **Leader regarding security needs** – your dog understands that you will decide what to do regarding perceived dangers and trusts your decisions.

3. **Leader who instigates interaction** – your dog understands that you decide when it is time to interact, and is relaxed when you leave and when you come in.

4. **Leader on the walk** – your dog understands it is you who instigates when to go on the walk, where you walk, and at what speed, and it follows.

Chapter 5
Your Dog's State

"Emotional self-control – delaying gratification and stifling impulsiveness – underlies accomplishment of every sort." (Daniel Goleman)

The bottom-up model

Adopting the language to demonstrate that you are a leader will ensure the dog looks to you for decisions regarding its wellbeing. However, there will be occasions when the dog will react impulsively to scenarios without conscious thought.

A dog's autopilot reaction can result in a heightened emotional state and leave it unable to process any further information. This will likely cause its behaviour to become problematic. Take a common example of a puppy that is jumping up and nipping people. In many cases, despite the guardian's best efforts to discourage it, the puppy's behaviour can become a real problem due to the puppy being overexcited and, as a result, unresponsive.

Understanding your dog's state in each moment is very important, as it will determine the likely behaviour that follows and the lessons that can be learnt, if any. A bottom-up model of behaviour can help us understand why a rise in state occurs and how to address the resulting behaviour with techniques such as associative learning and methods to teach self-control. This is useful because it will provide us with techniques to interrupt undesirable patterns of behaviour in order to get the dog's attention and teach it how to behave.

The trigger

A situation that causes the dog's state to alter, which in turn precipitates other behaviour, is known as a trigger. It can be a number of things, including getting out the lead or the vacuum cleaner, putting on your coat, saying goodbye to a family member, the postman coming to the door, the phone ringing, noise from outside, or the sight of another dog.

The meaning dogs give to stimuli depends on their internal representation of those stimuli. Therefore, a variety of feelings, such as excitement, nervousness, anxiety or curiosity, and different levels of state are created for each dog.

A dog's state in relation to a stimulus can be defined on a scale starting at 0, being the learning state in which it is calm and is responsive, going up to 10, at which point its state is completely heightened (fighting, shutting down from nerves, etc.).

When a stimulus is introduced, the dog's state rises to around 1–3 on the scale, where there are low levels of excitement, anxiety, nervousness or curiosity. At this point, the dog is aware of the stimulus but is calm and responsive. If the stimulus increases, comes closer and/or gains more meaning for the dog, the state is heightened to the next region, between 3 and 7 on the scale. At this point, the dog is focused on the stimulus and becomes less responsive to information. If the dog's state rises further, to between 7 and 10, then the dog is extremely focused on the stimulus rather than the guardian, and so is not capable of taking in any information.

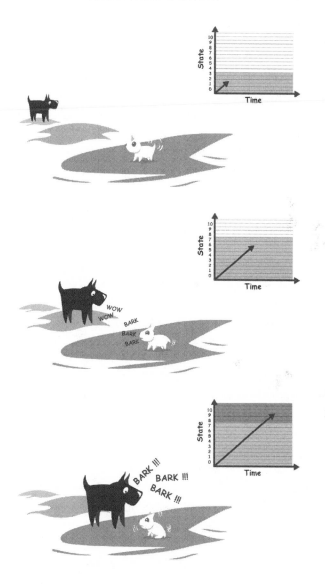

The trigger: an event that precipitates other events.

Through the dog's body language, we can see a wide variety of signs that indicate a rise in state. In the lower levels of the scale, we might see subtleties such as pricking up of ears or tail, focusing of eyes, or a change in pace or movement. At the medium level, there will be more active, unsettled movements, heavy panting, growling, barking, whining, avoidance behaviours such as walking away, or the dog may change its height with its tail and raise its hackles. At the top end of the scale, the body language accentuates and the behaviour becomes more erratic.

It is a common mistake to carry on with an action if the dog's state is heightened or rising, whatever the scenario. The Canadian neuroscientist Donald Hebb claims that *"cells that fire together, wire together"*, meaning that the more an action is repeated, the more the neural pathway strengthens and encodes patterns of behaviour in the brain. These negative responses occurring from a heightened state will eventually become habit if not addressed. A dog that has heightened experiences will then associate the events (the trigger) that lead up to the experience with a heightened response. For example, the dog can become overexcited each time it sees the lead, and carrying on without addressing the rise in state will likely result in more problems. The more the dog is allowed to have the same experience of heightened states related to certain places or situations, the more it is being inadvertently conditioned to behave in such a way.

These heightened states (3 and above) also affect the dog's health. When a dog perceives a situation as stressful, it releases a hormone called cortisol from the adrenal glands. This involves glucose being released from the dog's liver to provide energy to the muscles. This facilitates the flight, freeze or fight response to deal with the situation. A little amount irregularly is okay, but too much of this hormone being secreted over time is toxic to the dog's body. So exposing the dog to scenarios where its state is heightened must be avoided wherever possible.

Once we adjust our actions, only moving forward when the dog is in a calm state, we can produce new, desired behaviours. *The goal is to keep the dog calm, happy, and below a 3 on the scale.* Repeated experiences of this will boost the dog's confidence and create a new neural pathway in its brain, which can be strengthened to become habit.

Stages

Dogs learn from accumulated experiences, so we must ensure each experience is positive.

Ensuring that the dog feels safe, confident in its environment and responsive to your requests can be achieved by associative learning in stages. Processing information gradually is key for the lessons to be clear, and to not overwhelm and heighten the dog's state.

Although often, we do not consciously identify stages of learning, we regularly use them in our daily lives. For example, when learning to swim, we would not jump straight into the deep end, as that would be an advanced stage without the necessary foundations. The resulting experience would, more than likely, be a stressful one and knock our confidence in the water altogether. We may then resist any future event or associations that resemble the experience.

When we teach our children to swim, we first encourage them to go a short distance, such as half a metre, in the shallow end with the support of armbands. This helps them develop their technique and avoids stress. At each point, we address their safety needs by being there to look after them, whilst simultaneously addressing their belonging needs by demonstrating that we are the most experienced and should be looked to for guidance. And by taking it one step at a time, we are also taking into account the child's confidence/esteem needs. Once they are competent and confident in swimming half a metre, we encourage them to swim further and gradually progress over time, until they are swimming without armbands and for long distances, and do not need our help. Each distance can be identified as a stage, and how long each stage takes will differ between individuals. We must proceed at each individual child's pace, only moving forward once the pupil is in a relaxed state and the stage is complete. This ensures we take into account all their needs.

To teach a dog what we expect from them, again, we must go at their pace. This can be achieved by identifying stages for their learning development in each area. A first stage would be a starting point with minimal external stimuli, so that the dog is comfortable and receptive, looking to the guardian for information. As it learns a correct response, we gradually progress by introducing more external stimuli through each stage whilst reinforcing the learned response, to achieve the end goal with the dog's state never becoming heightened (always below a 3 on the scale). So, for example, when teaching a dog how to behave and return off the lead, the first stage would be to practise recall in the house where it is calm and we have their attention so it learns the correct response; the second stage would be to practise in the garden, then in a park on a long lead with no distractions, then introducing one distraction, and so on, whilst reinforcing the right response at each stage, until the dog can be off lead in the park with many other distractions.

Missing the necessary foundations of teaching and going straight to the park to let the dog off the lead can result in a heightened state from all the stimuli and, without the correct response having been taught, can create unpredictable behaviour. We have all seen guardians waiting, chasing or shouting to get their dogs to return. If, at any stage, the dog's behaviour becomes undesirable or it is not listening to you, it is necessary to identify and go back to the stage at which it was last listening, and progress from that point until you have the desired response.

Only once the desired result is achieved and the dog is calm and responsive is the stage complete. Then you are ready to move forward. Observe the dog's state closely in relation to its environment and plan each stage according to your surroundings, taking it one step at a time. There is no hurry.

The next natural step

The stages are applicable to everything you want the dog to learn. You can identify the beginning and end goals with a series of stages in between each area, be it food (being around picnics), the walk (as mentioned in Chapter 4), danger, separation, jumping up, etc.

Skipping the stages means missing out the foundations. Attempting to get a dog that is fearful to socialise with dogs in a park straight away can be a big ask. But if you take the time to allow the dog to feel comfortable walking at a distance from other dogs, and then gradually get closer as its state becomes calmer, you will be successful. Every time the dog has an experience, ideally, it will be in a calm state and the experience will be consistently positive. This will create new neural connections in the dog's brain related to its environment and your role. Over time, this will result in desirable patterns of behaviour and will help keep the dog in good health.

Interrupting the pattern

Lessons in stages will not always be perfect, as there will likely be surprises and scenarios that can cause the dog's state to rise, and it to react undesirably. In these moments, it is vital to know how to bring the dog's state back down to below a level 3, so the dog returns to being calm. This can be achieved with an action to interrupt its heightened state and change its focus. Once you have successfully interrupted its state, it will become receptive to further information. This will give you the opportunity to show it that you are present in the Guardian Role and teach it what it should be doing. This may take repeated attempts, especially if its behaviours have been allowed to develop into habit. However, the more you interrupt the negative patterns of behaviour, the more opportunities you have to create new, desired patterns.

You may previously have been advised to rattle stones or squirt the dog with a water pistol when it barks. This is an attempt to interrupt the dog's heightened state by distracting it so it loses its focus from a perceived threat. This method, like many other dog-training techniques, does not use language to reassure the dog that you are the decision-maker and will fulfil their needs. As a result, it seldom works in heightened situations when a dog has been used to protecting itself and the pack for a long time. In many cases, the dog learns to quickly ignore the distraction and carry on dealing with the danger because the guardians are not seen to be dealing with it.

To interrupt the dog's behaviour, and to be congruent with Guardian Role principles, it is important to a) always be seen to fulfil needs; and b) use forms of communication that will teach the dog to control its own behaviour. This way, the dog has the opportunity to reflect on its actions, see you in your role, and then choose to control its behaviour of its own free will.

Actions to reduce state

Below are a list of actions to reduce the dog's state, which in turn, will calm undesirable behaviour. Each action varies in how much it reduces the dog's state. The situation and level of your dog's state will dictate the action needed.

Not making eye contact with or speaking to the dog

Not making eye contact is a non-confrontational and clear way to say 'I don't want to interact yet' or 'You are not getting it right'. Most dogs will observe this language and realise they are not getting anywhere and will change their behaviour to respond appropriately. This message can be extended by turning your head and backing away from the dog.

Moving the dog away

Moving the dog away from a situation, by gently taking it by the collar without making eye contact, acts as a clear message that it is not needed. In many circumstances this will be enough for the dog to get the message and for its state to reduce, especially if the action is repeated a few times, with you gradually moving the dog further away each time. But in other scenarios, the dog may be in too much of a heightened state, which will require the next step of isolating.

Isolating the dog

Isolation involves gently taking the dog by the collar, without speaking to or looking at it, and putting it in another room so it cannot see you, giving it time to calm down. In isolation, the dog thinks to itself 'Where did that behaviour get me?' Once it is calm, it can rejoin the pack. These interruptions of behaviour, if repeated, will ensure the dog cannot maintain its heightened state. It will learn the consequence of its action by associating being calm and respectful with being let out, and behaving badly with being isolated. This consequence can be used for a range of unwanted behaviour inside the home, from invading your/your visitors' space, to play biting, to humping or stealing objects.

Not moving forward (stopping)

If your dog's state is rising, you may be able to stop whatever you are doing, whether it's picking up the lead, stopping moving on the walk, or refraining from throwing a ball. By not moving forward and waiting, you are allowing the dog's state to calm and giving it time to think about its actions.

Correcting a pull

When you correct a dog pulling by stopping, moving back a few steps and then waiting before moving forward, this briefly interrupts its action and gives time for its state to reduce.

Acknowledge the potential problem

By acknowledging the potential problem, you and your dog will be in communication with one another. In many cases (especially when you are accepted as leader), this will be enough for the dog to feel confident that you are fine with the situation and, as a result, to relax. If not, investigating the problem or choosing flight/curving/freeze may be required.

Flight

Choosing flight demonstrates that you are going to calmly walk away from whatever is making the dog's state rise. If done in time, the dog's state will not become heightened. The further you walk away from the trigger, the more quickly your dog's state will relax.

The curve

A variation on choosing flight is to curve. This involves walking to either side of a perceived danger until you pass it in a semi-circular motion. This will allow your dog to see that you are aware of the perceived danger and are reacting to it, by moving away to give sufficient distance.

The action of curving is also the ideal way to greet another dog. Walking straight towards another dog can make it very nervous. By curving, the other dog will see that your behaviour and your dog's is polite, that you wish to meet and that you are not threatening.

Calm freeze

If choosing flight is not possible, your next option is to use the calm freeze. This involves taking your dog by the collar, gently pulling it tightly into your body and putting yourself slightly in front of it. Once the dog relaxes, you can release your hold on it.

Checking

If your dog is not listening on the walk because it is distracted by smells, you can check the lead. This involves stopping, followed by gentle pulls upwards on the lead until the dog's focus is back to looking at you and the task in hand.

Reading and reacting

As soon as the dog's state rises, this is an opportunity to react. *Be sure to choose the appropriate response to reduce it, be that with a subtle or a more exaggerated action.* For example, if you are in the home and your dog is in the low levels of a heightened state and is invading your visitor's space, asking your visitor to adopt the golden five-minute ritual will likely be enough for the dog to get the message and leave them alone. But if your dog is in a more heightened state and demonstrates more erratic behaviour then a further action of moving the dog away or isolating may be necessary to calm it.

The options you have to reduce your dog's state change depending on your environment. For example, if you are outside with your dog and it is overly excitable when meeting other dogs, you will not have the option to isolate it. Here, you could wait or use the calm freeze to give your dog the opportunity to calm so it thinks about its actions. However, if your dog's state is above a 5 then walking it away until it calms may be necessary. Once your dog's state is calm, you can repeat the lesson by freezing or going back as many times as needed until your dog's state calms and it learns the correct way to greet and interact with dogs.

When first establishing your role as leader, many exaggerated movements may be necessary to reduce the dog's state – for example, walking away from perceived threats or putting your hands on the door when someone knocks on it. However, once you have proven yourself many times and your dog becomes more confident and calmer in their environment, they will notice your subtle gestures and feel at ease that you're in control. These gestures may include simply thanking the dog for alerting you to danger in the home without checking it out, or when out on a walk, changing your dog to your other side, away from a perceived danger. The more you are aware of the dog's state and know how to reduce it with either an exaggerated movement or subtle action, the more in sync you will become with them.

Rex's story

A client and now friend of mine called Stephanie asked me for help with her six-year-old terrier cross Rex, which she had recently rescued from Battersea Dogs & Cats Home. Stephanie explained that Rex was very well-behaved in the home but as soon as they went outside for a walk, he became stressed and would pull frantically on the lead and choke himself. As a result, the walk was not enjoyable for either of them.

We drew up a battle plan of how to address Rex's pulling behaviour in stages. This would ensure that Stephanie could teach him the response in a relaxed environment where he was calm and could gradually add more stimuli once he was responsive. We started where the walk begins, in the home. Stephanie showed me that Rex walked perfectly to heel in the house off lead and on lead. I wanted to watch Stephanie perfect the stop/start/change direction technique when Rex was pulling on the lead, so I suggested we continue on a quiet street outside as Stephanie did not have a garden.

As soon as we got outside onto the pavement, Rex's state heightened to an 8 on the scale and he immediately started pulling. Stephanie attempted to correct his pulling as instructed inside by stopping when he pulled, moving back a metre, waiting for him to calm (start) and moving forward. Rex, however, was not calming down or listening, and was pulling with all his strength. It took me 30 seconds to realise Rex was trying to pull to the side of the pavement as far away as possible from the oncoming traffic on the road. As soon as I spotted this, I asked Stephanie to stop correcting him and to walk quickly to the quiet street around the corner. As soon as we got to the quiet street, Rex's state immediately dropped from an 8 to a 4 and we had his attention in moments.

Suddenly, a new piece of the puzzle fell into place as to why Rex was panicking and pulling each time he went out. The trigger to his heightened state was the traffic, and that was the first thing he saw when he came outside. So when Stephanie took him for a walk to the park via this busy street, he was constantly in a heightened state and so was unable to be taught the correct response.

I explained to Stephanie that even though we know buses and cars on the road will not hurt us if we're on the pavement,

Rex did not know this and was attempting to get away from them. Any correcting at this point would cause resistance.

Stephanie understood, and from that moment on, she avoided putting Rex in any perceived danger to teach him the correct response. To do this, she allowed Rex to be as far away from the traffic as possible when walking to the quiet street. Once there, Rex was more relaxed, and every lesson further showed him that Stephanie was leading. This boosted his confidence and self-esteem. Many prolonged periods of calmness each time he was out rather than him being in a heightened state allowed positive patterns of behaviour to be formed. Gradually, once Rex was calm and responsive, Stephanie would go to slightly busier streets. If Rex's state began to heighten, she would walk back to the quiet street to interrupt his pattern of behaviour. Once he was calm, she would repeat the lesson. Each time she did this, she could walk a little bit longer with Rex on the busy street whilst he was in a calm state. Now, Stephanie can get from her front door to the park through all the busy streets without Rex's state rising.

Stephanie's location was not ideal for teaching Rex, as the busy road was the last stage for his learning development. Because of that, she had to plan the stages of the walk carefully to ensure Rex was not subjected to stress. This way, he could learn and could see Stephanie being active in her role as guardian.

Chapter 6
Leadership

"Example is leadership." (Albert Schweitzer)

The transformations I have witnessed in dogs initially displaying severely confused behaviour and transitioning to relaxed, responsive actions have always come down to the guardian striving to perfect communication. As the biggest influence on a dog's behaviour is its guardian and the situations he or she exposes the dog to, it is necessary to examine one's own qualities and the mindset it takes to become effective in the role of leader.

Leadership traits

The principal qualities needed to be a good leader of dogs are similar to the qualities needed to lead people. A parent/guardian whose leadership is inconsistent, controlling and quick to apportion blame for their mistakes is likely to be detrimental to development, whereas the well-mannered, consistent, gentle, firm but fair guardian is likely to contribute to healthy development. Both can be considered leaders due to the situations dogs and children find themselves in, but a chaotic, inconsistent leadership style will be confusing and therefore questioned on a regular basis through undesirable behaviour. To give the dog the best chance to learn, a leader who is calm, convincing and consistent in their actions is needed.

Calm

The dog's behaviour is affected by the guardian's response in each situation. A dog that sees its guardian remaining calm will assess the language and actions triggered by a situation and will think 'The leader is calm; I trust him/her, so there is no need for concern.' If the guardian is stressed, the dog will pick up on their body language and state and will also become agitated. Once the dog's state becomes heightened, the message the guardian wishes to convey will be compromised. If at any point you become stressed, it is better to avoid the situation until you feel calm again. Short lessons when both you and the dog feel happy will allow the experiences to be more enjoyable and productive for you and your dog.

Convincing

Being convincing in the role of guardian can take some practice. You may be communicating that you are the needs fulfiller by adopting the four areas, but how well that message is relayed is varied. There is a big difference between a dog being safe and feeling safe, or between a dog having confidence in your abilities in some areas or in every area. For the dog to truly see you as leader, they must intrinsically understand that you are the food provider and get priority feeding, that you deal with all danger, that you decide when it is time to interact, and that you lead the walk. As you acquire the language and step up to the role, a natural learning process involves four stages:

1. Unconscious incompetence – you are unaware of what you do not know.

2. Conscious incompetence – you are aware of what you do not know.
3. Conscious competence – you are competent in the role, but have to consciously think about it.
4. Unconscious competence – you are competent and do not have to consciously think about it.

This learning process can be illustrated by the example of learning to drive. In the first stage of learning, i.e. as a child, you are unaware of what the concept of driving entails. In the second stage, you are aware of what driving entails, but know you do not know how to drive. The third stage involves you learning to drive, but having to consciously think about what you are doing at all times. The fourth stage is when you can drive the car without having to consciously think about it and the action becomes second nature.

Regarding dogs and leadership, when you are at the third stage of learning and still have to think about what you are doing, many dogs will be convinced that you are taking charge but some will remain unconvinced. For example, a guardian trying to withhold reuniting after a separation whilst staring at the ceiling and saying, 'I am not talking to you' through their teeth will not convince every dog. Rather, it is at the last stage of unconscious competence that your language will convince the tougher cases that you know what you are doing in the role.

Consistent

For the dog to learn a correct response, consistency is paramount. As the dog learns in stages, consistency will help it understand what is expected from it in each area. Remember that all four areas need to be done together and consistently.

Nothing will confuse a dog more than inconsistency, and if there are other family members, friends or dog-walkers being inconsistent with the language and lessons you are teaching, the dog will receive mixed messages and the whole process will take longer or might even fail altogether.

The area with which most people typically struggle is point 3 – their status of leader (golden five minutes, invitation only, and do not go up to the dog). If your status as leader is not communicated then addressing other issues can be a constant battle.

Knowing the dog's language and responding in a calm, convincing and consistent manner will allow the dog to recognise your competence in the role. It will then only be a matter of time and accumulated positive experiences until the dog elects you in charge.

Management

A common question asked is 'How long will the process take for the dog to elect the guardian as leader?' The answer is that each case will be different due to a multitude of factors such as the guardian's leadership skills, how many lessons are put in, if those lessons are clear, other people's influence, the severity of the problem, previous experiences, lack of resources, the dog's nature, etc. Some processes may take days whilst others may take months. *It is very important to remember that we must go at the dog's pace, not ours.* However, communicating your role effectively and providing good management in each situation will speed up the progress.

Create lessons

You can speed up the process by actively putting in more lessons in each area. For example, if your dog invades your visitors' personal space when they enter the home, you could invite a lot of people round and ask them to withhold communicating with the dog. If your dog jumps up, you could isolate it and ask your visitor to go out and come back in again to give your dog another lesson. Or if your dog has separation anxiety, you can walk in and out of the room or the house many times throughout the day, building the amount of time you are gone. Or if you are trying to teach your dog to walk to heel, going for more walks means more lessons.

Clear lessons

For each lesson to be clear, we need the dog to consciously think and learn what you are teaching it. The dog will not understand the message if they are in a heightened state or preoccupied with something else, or if they are being controlled, distracted or restricted. For example, if you are restricting the dog's access to upstairs by using a barrier then do not expect them to have learnt that they cannot go upstairs. Rather, they will just have been physically not able to go upstairs. It is fine to have a barrier in this instance, as it does not affect your role, but if you want to teach them that upstairs is a no-go zone, you could remove the barrier and correct them each time they attempt to go up by bringing them down again. If they persist, you could isolate them each time they go up. This way, they are free to experience what you are teaching and then make the conscious choice not to go upstairs.

If you have two dogs, and it becomes a struggle to communicate that you are dealing with danger because their barking is winding each other up, you could put one dog in another room, or ask a friend or family member to look after it for a few hours, and practise with the other one individually. You could ask a family member to knock on the door a number of times throughout the day so you start to see the changes in quick succession. Once you have put in some lessons and seen changes, repeat the lessons with the other dog and build up until you can put them both together. This will give the dogs the necessary time to process your teachings.

Quality lessons

It is more important that each lesson is about quality rather than duration. A quality lesson involves you feeling positive and raring to go, your dog being happy and the lesson being clear. These lessons, if done correctly, all head in the right direction.

Be sure not to set yourself up for failure by instigating a lesson in which you are not in the right frame of mind to address it properly. For example, if you are short of time and are taking the dog with you on the school run and it starts pulling, you will likely become frustrated and rush because you have to get to the school in time. The lesson becomes counterproductive. In this situation, it is best to leave the dog at home or otherwise, be prepared to leave early for school so you can answer each pull without time pressures. Another solution could be to go on a dry run to school with your child and the dog on the weekend, when you are free from time pressure. Once you have seen how long it takes to get to school, this will give you an idea of how much time you need on a normal day. Simply put, if you have not got the time to put in the right lessons then wait for a time when you do.

If lessons are too long, you will lose your dog's focus and suffer a setback. So gauge when you start to lose their attention and cut it short before that happens. Keep the lessons fun and the right length.

Other people

The right communication has to be continuous with all the people your dog has regular contact with for lessons to be consistent. It is of course not always possible to get every family member to convincingly adopt the Guardian Role principles, so at the very least, if it is only you who is effectively communicating with your dog, you will still see progress. But the more people on board, the more relaxed the dog will be.

Over the years, clients have proclaimed that they have had to become quite firm with some visitors, understanding that their dog's progress would be helped or hindered as a result of their actions. The dog's guardian would tell visitors what they should do, i.e. not to invade the dog's space, withhold from greeting for a period of time, interact on your terms, etc. The majority of people in these situations are very helpful, and as a result, the guardians welcome their interaction, but some people, even with the best intentions, ignore the guardian's requests.

In the latter scenario, it is best to avoid the wrong lessons. For example, in the case of visitors coming to the home, you could put the dog in another room for the duration of their visit or, if it is someone who is staying over for a while or a frequent visitor you are determined to educate, you could call or text them beforehand to remind them what to do before they come over. Once they arrive, remind them again. If they do not get it right by looking at or talking to the dog, you can ask them to go out and come back in, and remind them this time to do it properly until the dog leaves them alone. You should only have to isolate your visitors once before they understand the rule!

Many guardians will have dog sitters, boarders or walkers to look after the dog and, again, the situation requires them to carry on the right communication in their absence. One client changed their dog boarders a few times, as problems kept occurring each time the dog was returned, until they found someone who was willing to listen.

Another guardian, who had a dog with aggression issues towards other dogs, managed the dog's experiences when she was at work by postponing her dog walker. The dog was getting into negative patterns of behaviour each time it was out with the dog walker, as he was not able to put in lessons due to having many dogs with him. So the guardian employed a dog sitter to take care of the dog when she went to work. The dog sitter came to the house to let the dog out for the toilet and to play in the garden, but not for a walk. This gave the dog some respite from the problems and the negative patterns of behaviour. Once the guardian got home, she then put in the lessons, showing that she would provide for the dog's needs, and new, positive patterns of behaviour formed. Once this good behaviour became a habit, she relayed some instructions to the dog walker and now the dog is walking in the pack again without any issues.

Some dog lovers (and this has probably happened to you) will come up to your dog and pet them without asking. The person will not understand the potential consequence of their actions if your dog suffers from nervous or aggressive issues. It can also provoke problem behaviours with many dogs, as they will not always understand the person's kind intentions. So it is best to avoid these situations by kindly telling the person that the dog doesn't like being approached, whilst manoeuvring it out of the way or placing yourself in front of it (freezing). It may upset the person but that is better than them being bitten or your dog being frightened. After you have stopped the person, you can explain why.

Once you have explained, if the person is still keen to interact with your dog, you could use it as an opportunity for another lesson and ask them to call your dog into their space. *Instruct the person not to invade the dog's space at any point.* If the dog is happy to go to them and the person is respectful of the dog's space then it will be a positive experience; if the dog does not move then they are clearly saying they are not comfortable and so must be left alone until they are ready.

I go into detail on how to manage children with regard to dogs in Chapter 20.

Other people's dogs

You will at some point likely come across people who allow their dog to misbehave and pester your dog. It is an impossible task to effectively manage other people's actions in these scenarios, but what you can do is aim to have maximum control of your dog in any given situation in order to avoid negative experiences where possible.

The first thing is to make sure your dog's recall is brilliant when around other dogs. This will enable you to call them back if another dog appears a nuisance, and to walk in the opposite direction to them. The second thing to do is to read the other dog's language and how the person appears to be with their dog from afar. If the guardian does not appear to have control of their dog, there will be some telltale signs such as barking, pulling on the lead, eyes bulging, running around frantically whilst not listening to its guardian, etc. So if you spot any of these signs, avoid these dogs and their guardians by walking in a different direction.

If, in any of these scenarios, the dog comes over to your dog, you can continue fleeing by walking out of the park or into a safe area. If the dog catches up with you, you then have the option of freezing. In this scenario, you can calmly interact with the other dog, whilst you call the guardian to come and retrieve it.

Managing the home

There are often areas in the home environment where the dog acquires undesirable patterns of behaviour that can hinder the process: for example, a place where they attempt to escape or habitually bark when the guardian leaves, a room with objects they can chew, etc. These areas can be modified, blocked off or altered in order to manage the situation.

You can manage the house in many ways:

- You can move objects out of reach that the dog jumps up to steal.
- If you have dogs that are really small, you could put them on a lead when you anticipate problem behaviour, in order to get a hold of them if necessary.
- You can cover up little crevices that the dog will hide in to escape from you.
- You can put chairs on the sofa when you leave the house so the dog cannot get on top and bark out of the window at people walking past.

- If your dog is chewing objects in the home every time you leave, make sure there is nothing valuable for them to chew on.
- If your dog toilets in the home then put something down, or pick up the rug to limit damage.

Whatever the problem, there is always something that can be modified so you can manage the situation.

Myrtle's story

Myrtle was constantly active in trying to protect the house, and would bark and run from one end of the home to the other throughout the day. Each time she would bark at a perceived danger, her owner, May, would check it out. However, May was often too late, as Myrtle would then run to other side of the home, barking to deal with another perceived danger. So the message that May was protecting the home was not clear to Myrtle.

I arrived at May's home to see that the house was very big and Myrtle was very small. As a result, Myrtle was able to run circles around May. I explained to May that we had to alter the environment so Myrtle could see her in her role as protector. First, we restricted Myrtle's access to certain areas so she could not slip past May anymore. We made sure doors were closed and used baby gates where appropriate. This ensured that May and Myrtle were always in close proximity to each other. Now, each time Myrtle sounded the alarm, May was in a position to respond effectively. This allowed Myrtle to learn that May was aware of the danger and was dealing with it. Once Myrtle was convinced of May's leadership in one room, May would open up access to another and demonstrate leadership there. May continued to gradually extend Myrtle's space as she accepted that her guardian was dealing with any perceived danger until the house was back to normal, without any baby gates or doors closed. Myrtle is now in the habit of looking for May's response, wherever the danger is.

Attention to detail

There can be times during the interaction between guardian and dog where the message of 'who is instructing whom' is unclear. These moments stem from the dog's subtle behaviours, which manipulate the guardian in a way that goes unnoticed. The guardian asks the dog to do something but the message is regularly ignored. In all cases, it is better to really observe, from the dog's perspective, what is going on in each situation and check how you are coming across, ensuring that you give off the correct signals.

Routines

Resist a rigid routine with your dog's daily activities, as they can become conditioned to the timing and end up initiating a response from you. For example, if you get up at a certain time each day and the first thing you do is feed your dog, who happens to be there waiting and staring at you, the dog can think it is telling you to feed them and you are responding. In other words, they think they are controlling you! A similar situation can arise if you go for walks at certain times each day. In such cases, wait for them to settle first and, once they have left you alone, you can then initiate the walk, play, attention or feed to make it clear you are making the decisions each time.

Furniture

Having your dogs on the furniture is a personal choice. It may suit you or it may not. I personally allow my dog on the couch and on my bed. However, it is by invitation only. It is best to make sure you call your dog up on the furniture, rather than allowing it to just jump up when it decides to. If the dog jumps up on the couch and then after 10 minutes, is on your lap being stroked without being invited, it *may have* unconsciously manoeuvred you into this, sending a compromising signal in status: who decides when it is time to interact? In order to avoid incorrect messages and to make things black-and-white, a rule could be that the dog is not allowed on the couch unless you ask it up there. That way, you are more likely to notice your dog's subtler, unconscious advances.

Toys

Many guardians have lots of toys for their dog lying around the home, expecting that the dog will happily play with them on their own. In truth, I seldom see a dog playing with a toy on its own. I usually see it either destroy the toy or grab it after each separation and throughout the day to manoeuvre the guardian into play. The dog will often parade it around the home and approach or stare at the guardian as if to say 'Look what I have, acknowledge me.' If that is the case with your dog, it is best to remove the opportunity to do this by presenting the toy when you decide it is time to play and then putting it away after you decide playtime is over. This will avoid toys being destroyed and any confusion over who decides when it is time to play and interact.

Show your dog

Much like when correcting the dog pulling on lead to show it the desired position it should be in, when asking your dog to do something, be sure to show it what you mean. For example, if you want to get your dog out of the kitchen, first say 'away' and point towards where you want it to go. If it does not move away, gently take it by the collar and show it what you mean (repeating the request of 'away'), and release their collar once you have taken it to where you want it to be.

If you fall into the trap of resorting to saying something five times and the dog appears to be disobeying the request then consider the possibility it might not know what you mean. You'll likely become frustrated if you say something five times and your request is being ignored. In these moments, if the dog does not understand you, your voice will become like white noise; if you become further agitated, you will look as if you have lost control. So it is best to say things once, calmly, and maybe say it again if the dog does not respond; then gently show it with your body language what it should be doing. This gives you the opportunity to teach your dog what your body language, tone and words mean. Over time, your dog will associate the words with an action, listen to you and respond straight away.

Never get angry or shout; just keep showing your dog until it gets it. The chances are if you are often talking, you are getting it wrong. Remember, it's 90 per cent body language and 10 per cent words and tone.

Also, never beg, plead or pander to your dog. Great leaders are convincing and consistent, and are all about calm actions.

Mindset

The ability to address a dog's undesirable behaviour is part knowledge, part action and part mindset. The next section explores some of the common beliefs that could limit your potential, and gives tips on how to get into the right mindset to get results.

Age

Everyone has heard the phrase 'You cannot teach an old dog new tricks'. The statement is simply not true. The person who originally said this has played a part in influencing many failures with dogs and people all around the world.

So often, clients ask me, 'My dog is X years old; is it too late to correct their behaviour?' To answer this question, I mention one client who had a twelve-year-old dog, to whom they successfully managed to communicate their position, making a significant change in their behaviour. Dogs can get set in their ways, as can people, granted, but whilst a dog is healthy and responsive, they are always capable of learning something new. I have found that some older dogs who have exhibited undesirable behaviour for some time can improve faster than younger canines – there is no real pattern!

Breed

We hear all sorts of information on behaviour that is specific to the breed of dog. This is often followed up with an excuse as to why behaviour cannot be corrected: for example, beagles run away because they are scent hounds, and so get carried away when they pick up a smell; huskies will not walk to heel, because they were bred to pull sledges; terriers are aggressive because they were bred to hunt.

These statements assume the traits are bred into the dog's nature and so the behavioural problems cannot be resolved. Thinking that the traits are inherent will limit your belief that it is possible to correct the behaviour. Granted, certain breeds often have individuals with similar traits. This may or may not influence behaviour. However, no matter what the breed of dog, with the right nurture, they can all be taught to be well-behaved in the areas required: being socially acceptable around people and other dogs, walking to heel, coming back when called, being calm and responsive in all situations, e.g. when you arrive or leave, etc. In short, rest assured, your dog's behavioural problems can be resolved, whatever the breed.

Mind-reading

One client believed her dog was toileting in the house to annoy her. This belief made her angry, which in turn meant she had a lack of patience with her dog and found it hard to address the problem in a calm fashion. Once she stopped falsely mind-reading the dog's intentions and understood that the behaviour originated from one or more of the dog's attempts to fulfil its needs, she understood her dog on a deeper level and was able to address the issue without harbouring ill feelings.

Another client thought his dog didn't like him because the dog would bark at him and run to his girlfriend each time he came home or moved towards it. His reaction was simply not to care because there had been no chance for he and the dog to bond. He thought, 'Why bother?' But after he learnt that his body language was intimidating the dog when he would approach it, just by going up to the dog and stroking it, he was keen to learn and demonstrate non-confrontational signals to rebuild the relationship. And he did.

I have heard a number of people trivialise their dogs' stressed barking behaviour with comments such as 'He just likes his own voice', and 'He knows I'm coming home, he is just protesting'. This incorrect mind-reading often leads to the guardians not even attempting to address the issues.

In each situation, seeking to understand the real reasons behind the behaviour – the dog's unmet needs – rather than mind-reading, will give you more patience and lead you to an effective course of action.

Rescue dogs

Many wonderful people rescue dogs from centres or other people. All of these dogs are desperate to please and want to stay in their new homes. The majority find happiness without many problems. However, sometimes behavioural problems, based on confusion about who their leader is, causes them to be rehomed many times or, in the worst-case scenario, meet tragic ends.

Those who own a rescue dog with behavioural problems often attempt to piece together a violent or neglectful history to explain the bad behaviour. In some cases, the guardians may know this to be true or guess right, but in other cases, their explanations are wrong.

Trying to guess the previous experiences your dog might have gone through to explain its present behaviour will help with patience and empathy, which will help with your mindset. However, this way of thinking can be a double-edged sword, which may cause people to believe that the dog's behaviour will never change due to its past. If a rescue dog has had a traumatic past, it may take longer before the dog becomes confident that you will provide for them. But what has happened in its past does not equal its future.

Dogs think in the 'present moment' more than we do, so it is more important to concentrate and ask questions regarding solution-focused thinking, e.g. when does the problem behaviour begin? What can we do to show them we will provide for them? How can we accumulate a series of positive experiences? How can we show them we can be trusted? etc. This will put us in the empowering frame of mind to answer these questions. If you focus on the solution to each problem and believe all dogs can change, it will enable you to help the severest of cases.

I should add that there are many rescue dogs of all breeds, ages and sizes waiting to be rehomed that do not have any behavioural problems. The great thing about rescuing a dog is that you can see what personality you are getting, as well as getting an age and size that suits you.

Questions and answers

We can take the emotions, presuppositions and false beliefs out of the equation by simplifying our approach and acknowledging each behaviour as a question. Each time your dog jumps up, pulls on the lead, toilets in the home, shows aggression, steals belongings, puts its paw on you, stands on you, doesn't listen to you, doesn't come back when asked, whines at you, barks at you or barks when you leave, see it as a question that needs answering. Throughout the day – question, question, question.

Your dog has to ask questions so they can understand what they have control over and what they must look to you for. It is not important how many times your dog asks the question; what matters is how you answer. These answers, delivered calmly, convincingly and consistently, all add up to good lessons. It is only a matter of time until your dog gets the message.

Test of wills

If you have a particularly challenging dog, they will test you time and time again. Addressing these behaviours can come down to who has the strongest will, you or your dog. Show your dog that it is you by always being prepared to go that one step further.

Measuring progress

Whatever the situation, it is key that you realistically measure your dog's progress so that your own confidence grows. It can become very demotivating when you believe it is not working. However, there will be occasions when progress does not seem to be happening but it actually is.

In whatever area you are teaching your dog, if the stages appear too big, they can be reduced to *checkpoints* within that stage. Reducing the goal to small segments will allow you to recognise the subtlest of progress. For example, if you are trying to teach your dog to walk to heel outside then you could first identify a checkpoint near your house, such as a tree, and try to get there without your dog pulling on the lead. Once you have got there without a pull, attempt to get to the next tree. Each time you get pulled return to the previous checkpoint until you have passed the next one successfully. This way, you can count how many times you are being pulled and come back and improve if necessary. We always have to start somewhere and then build the information in, no matter how insignificant the starting point may be. *Stages and checkpoints will not only boost your dog's confidence but also your confidence that what you are doing is working.*

Bertie's story

A client called Sarah had a dog called Bertie. Sarah called me in because Bertie was hyperactive on the walk and would pull to the point where he would strangle himself.

I explained to Sarah how to communicate her role to Bertie and told her not to take him out that day, but instead to practise getting him to walk by her side without the lead in the house. Sarah began and showed me some progress by walking around the house with Bertie following her perfectly off lead. I then asked her to call Bertie over, calmly put the lead on and walk around the house with him by her side for a short distance. Bertie appeared uncomfortable with the lead on. Sarah began walking and he shot ahead, pulling the lead taut. I asked Sarah to stop, turn around, wait a few seconds and try again. This time, Bertie walked with Sarah for a split second, but again, shot forward. Once again, I asked Sarah to stop, turn around, wait a few seconds and repeat the action. Sarah got Bertie in position and tried again, but after she took a couple of steps, he still shot forward.

This happened a few more times until Sarah looked at me and in a distressed voice said, 'It's not working; he's never going to get it!' I told her it was working right there in front of her. I explained to her that each time, there had been some progress. The first time, Bertie had walked four steps before shooting forward, then six steps, then eight, and so on. Because of his size, his little legs moved so fast that it was hard to see the progress, but it was there. Sarah then felt reassured and continued. Twenty-plus attempts and resets later, Sarah and

Bertie were walking up and down her small front room with no pulling. There is always progress to be made when you reduce the goal to tiny, manageable checkpoints. In this case, they were to walk for a quarter of a metre without a pull, then half a metre, then one metre, and so on. Sarah had to show Bertie how to walk a metre about 10 times, but eventually, he got it and progressed. As Sarah learned to establish checkpoints in stages, she became confident in her abilities and in Bertie's capability to get it right.

Change the words for different meaning

Words have different meanings for, and provoke different reactions from, each individual. The meaning an individual applies to the word can either hinder or help their mindset. For example, asking your visitors to ignore your dog when they enter the home could result in them feeling like they are being rude. For human beings, if you ignore somebody, it is usually associated with a negative response. As a result, visitors will have internal, conflicting views on what they have been asked to do, making it hard for them to do it. In these cases, you won't always have time to explain what your dog is really doing when it is jumping up on the visitor or bringing objects to them. In situations like these, a helpful tip is to ask your visitor to wait until the dog is calm and leaves you alone, but then greet them as enthusiastically as they like. That way, you will face less resistance.

Another example of changing the meaning of something to make it easier can be used on the walk. The word 'walk' makes you think of an enjoyable experience with your dog, getting some fresh air and socialising with others, usually in a nice park. If your dog is difficult when you go out, it can become extra frustrating due to the picture you created in your head.

A change of words can help you get in the right mindset. You can say to yourself, whatever the scenario – be it that your dog is fearful of a situation, pulls on the lead, becomes over excited, etc. – that you are concentrating on boosting your dog's confidence so they respond in a desirable manner. This way, you will visualise what the work entails (stages) and you will become more focused and less frustrated by managing your expectations.

Envisage the end goal

To ensure a high standard of your dog being happy and well-behaved, and looking to you for guidance in each part of their life, remember: *the dog must intrinsically understand that you are making the decisions in those four areas.* So keep communicating to your dog that you want it to eat all its food without any fuss; to look to you when confronted by perceived dangers, and relax once you have acknowledged/dealt with them; to be respectful of your personal space, as well as that of your visitors and also strangers; and to walk to heel by following your pace and direction, coming to you each time you call them. Once this is achieved, their eyes soften and they will be calm, relaxed and responsive in every environment.

If you identify your dog's needs, communicate your status, plan the necessary stages (and checkpoints within the stages if necessary), instigate clear lessons and manage the environment well – staying calm, convincing and consistent as you work towards the end goal in each area – you will get there.

"Leadership and learning are indispensable to each other." (John F. Kennedy)

The following chapters are made up of case studies, documenting my clients and my personal experiences of working with dogs.

The studies reveal in detail how we addressed more specific problem behaviours using the Guardian Role principles explained in the previous four chapters – identifying the dog's needs, communicating that it is the guardian who is providing for the dog's needs (the four areas), teaching the dog in stages, understanding their state and how to influence it by interrupting negative patterns of behaviour, and how one can become a calm, convincing, consistent leader whom the dog trusts.

I have been fortunate to work closely with many clients and their dogs for both short, one-off consultations and long holiday periods. During the clients' absence, I would stay in their homes and look after their dogs whilst communicating my role as their temporary guardian. Once the clients returned, I advised them on how to carry on. Each time, the dog demonstrated a clear difference in behaviour before and after the holiday, and so the clients were motivated to continue the new forms of communication. The new responses the dog learned were, the majority of the time, transferable, providing that the owner continued to put in the lessons from where I left off. However, in some cases, the dog would assess the owner's behaviour and would not be convinced of their leadership, so the behaviour would slip back.

Through my time providing these services, I have encountered a variety of different undesirable behaviours. Some cases were extreme, which at times, caused me to struggle. In turn, I doubted the effectiveness of the communication. But the following stories reveal how the challenging cases taught the clients and me to constantly reflect and adapt our leadership when needed. When I look back, it was the most challenging cases that taught me the most.

Each dog always had more than one problem but, to keep things simple, I will talk about the applicable problem in each case to avoid sounding repetitive.

PART 3
CASE STUDIES

Chapter 7
Issues With Food

Food is the dog's most precious commodity; without it, they will die. If the dog is assuming they have power or is questioning their role in this area, they typically exhibit undesirable behaviours such as refusing to eat, whining to be fed, aggression around food, invading people's space when they eat, and stealing food.

Sophie's story

Trudy and Steven were the guardians to a food-obsessed Labrador named Sophie. Sophie had developed an undesirable pattern of behaviour of barking each time her food was being prepared. She also stole food at every opportunity from Trudy and Steven, as well as people having picnics in the park.

Trudy and Steven had been dealing with Sophie's behaviour by shutting her in another room each time they ate a meal. And they never visited parks on sunny days to avoid the picnickers. They had come to the realisation that their lives were revolving around Sophie's problem behaviour, so they called me for help.

After hearing the problems they were experiencing with Sophie, I explained that Sophie's problem behaviour was due to a misunderstanding of her position in the family. As a result, she was unclear about the rules around food. I explained the 'Guardian Role' principles and how gesture eating is used as a statement to communicate one's leadership position around food.

I asked Trudy to feed Sophie in front of me and gesture eat so I could observe Sophie's behaviour. Trudy began preparing the food and Sophie jumped on her. I asked Trudy to push her down without speaking or looking. Sophie then began whining and barking, so I instructed Trudy to stop what she was doing and wait for Sophie to be quiet before she continued. Sophie went quiet, so Trudy continued preparing the food, but a moment later, Sophie barked again so Trudy stopped. This happened a few more times until I instructed Trudy to walk off the next time Sophie barked. Sure enough, Sophie barked again, so Trudy abandoned feeding her. After a few minutes, Trudy returned to feeding her, but this time, Sophie learned to control her behaviour and was quiet whilst Trudy prepared the food. Trudy then gesture ate and gave Sophie her food.

I then asked Steven to make himself something to eat so I could see Sophie's attempts to steal his food. Steven made a sandwich and sat down at the table to eat it. Sophie came up to the table in a boisterous manner and jumped on him, so I instructed Steven to push her away without speaking or looking at her. This did not have the desired effect as she jumped straight back on Steven. So I asked Steven to make the message clearer by taking Sophie by the collar and moving her away 10 feet, releasing her and then returning to the table (all without speaking or looking at her). Steven did this and Sophie immediately returned to get to the sandwich. I pointed out to Steven that we needed to make the message clearer, so I asked him to isolate Sophie in the bathroom. Steven did this and left her in there to give her time to calm down (about 20 seconds) before letting her out. When Steven let Sophie out, she ran back to the table to get to the sandwich so Steven isolated her again, but this time, for 30 seconds. This scenario was repeated another 15 times, with Steven isolating Sophie for a little longer each time before letting her out, until she got the message not to approach Steven whilst he was eating at the table. Trudy and Steven looked delighted with the result. Steven then ate his food with Sophie in the room for the first time in a year without disturbance.

I explained to Trudy and Steven that the foundations must be strong in the home before meeting picnickers, so we instigated lessons by sitting on the sofa to eat food to see if Sophie would come over. Sophie did not approach, so they went a stage further by eating their lunch sitting on the floor. This time, Sophie could not resist investigating, so Trudy and Steven took turns to respond by moving her away or isolating her if necessary until she learnt not to come over whilst they were eating. Patience and persistence are always vital.

Over the following days, Trudy and Steven invited friends around and had their version of a picnic on the floor to teach Sophie more lessons around food. Once Sophie understood to never invade anyone's personal space when they were eating, no matter where they ate, they took it a stage further by taking Sophie out to the park where they knew there would be picnickers, but on a long lead so they could correct her if she got it wrong. But Sophie did not approach anyone eating food. The lessons in the home translated to the outside world. Trudy and Steven took her off the long lead and they are now all free to enjoy their walks in busy parks around picnickers without any trouble.

Added tips:

- Feed your dog when you want. It does not matter when you eat; this is about showing your dog each time it is being fed that you have priority feeding.

- Do not feed your dog as a direct result of it looking at you. Otherwise, it will become confused as to who is telling whom when mealtimes are.

- Never go up to your dog when it is eating; its personal space must be respected.

- Do not look at your dog when it is eating; this takes the pressure off it.

- If your dog is pestering you when you have your own food, be sure to put in the appropriate lesson.

- In the wild, leaders do not necessarily eat first, especially if their physiological needs are already met. However, the important thing to remember is they can eat first if they choose to and other wolves are aware of this. Gesture eating is a statement to communicate your position. Once your dog understands you are the leader and so are entitled to priority feeding, you can stop gesture eating.

- Remember, if your dog does not finish all its food, pick the bowl up and do not feed your dog until it is time for its next meal. Do not worry; a dog will never starve itself to death.

- Watch the video tutorial on my website.

Chapter 8
Dogs and Perceived Dangers

"A dog wants to feel safe or in control, but will only give up control once it feels safe." (Nigel Reed)

All dogs have their own perception of what is and what is not safe. If the dog does not perceive the guardian to be taking care of perceived danger, they will be forced to provide for their own safety needs using one of the three Fs. Here's an example of each one.

Flight

Scooby's story

Toby and Margaret were the guardians to a Great Dane called Scooby. Scooby had a few problems but the main one was his refusal to go into the vets. As soon as they had Scooby near the vets, he would resist going in. If he was forced, he would overpower Toby and Margaret and run off and hide. Toby and Margaret tried different leads, luring him with food, and even using a different veterinary practice, but Scooby always saw through their tactics and would resist going in.

I explained to them why the problem was happening and how Scooby was making the decisions for his own safety; he simply perceived the vets as unsafe so he refused to go in. I explained that if Scooby trusted their decision-making, he would follow wherever they decided to go. From here on, we would have to ensure the experience was not traumatic for him. After I advised them on what to do, Toby and Margaret were enthusiastic and keen to communicate their role to Scooby.

They began going through the stages of the walk and putting lessons in to communicate that they were leading. Toby and Margaret lived close to the vets but each time they went for a walk, they avoided walking past it so Scooby would not become concerned and feel the need to take control. After a couple of weeks, they told me they were at the stage of walking past the vets without any struggle, but were not going to go in just yet as they did not want to push it. A week later, they would go to the vets and open the door, but not go in. After a couple days of doing this, they walked into the practice with Scooby and asked the receptionist to greet him with a treat once he was settled. Each walk and visit was designed to accumulate positive experiences for Scooby and to avoid setbacks. Toby and Margaret repeated going into the vets for five days, building up to an appointment booked the following week. When it was time for the appointment, Scooby walked into the practice and to the consultation room confidently. The vet gave him a check-up, prescribed some medication and sent them on their way.

I was impressed by how Margaret and Toby had dealt with the situation. They knew their goal, never lost sight of it and worked towards it each day without using any force. As a result, Scooby never resisted them and he now trusts their decisions in every area.

Freeze

Fred's story

A very stressed Border Collie named Fred lived with his guardians, Sally and Mark. Each time the doorbell rang, Fred would quickly go into autopilot and bark furiously. When visitors came into the home, Fred would become extremely nervous and bark if they moved. Sally and Mark were becoming increasingly worried that Fred's barking would turn into aggression, as he appeared to be becoming more distraught and confrontational with each visitor.

I knocked on Sally and Mark's door and heard Fred barking. Sally invited me in and Mark had Fred (as requested) on a lead. Fred was not happy with my presence and was lunging and barking, so I asked Mark to put him in another room, shut the door and come back in without him. Mark isolated Fred in the kitchen, where he carried on barking.

I explained to Mark and Sally that whilst Fred was stressed, it was very hard for him to take in any information. The isolating gave him time to calm down. I requested that, as soon as soon Fred's state reduced and he stopped barking, Mark should go and get him without saying a word and walk him back into the room whilst looking at me and talking in a relaxed voice. If Fred barked, I wanted Mark to put him straight back in the kitchen and close the door so he learned the consequence of his action.

Fred was in the kitchen barking for a good 10 minutes before he calmed down. At this point, Mark got him and brought him back into the room. Fred took one look at me and barked again, so Mark quickly took him out and isolated him. Fred carried on barking, but for around seven minutes this time. As soon as he stopped, Mark went and got him again. This time, Fred looked at me but paused for 10 seconds before he barked. Mark again put him out. I explained to Mark and Sally that he was processing the information and learning the consequence of his action. Over time, he would realise his behaviour was not getting him anywhere, and eventually, he would stop completely. We repeated this process about 30 times, with Fred's barks becoming less intense each time he saw me, until he was not barking at all when in isolation. Mark went and got Fred again and, this time, when he came in, he lay down by Mark's feet. He had given in. Sally and Mark looked relieved. This was the first time in months that he had been relaxed with a visitor in the room.

The next job was to tackle Fred's reaction at the door, so I told Sally and Mark what to do when the doorbell rang (thank, look and if necessary, isolate). I asked Mark to go outside and knock on the door to elicit a response from Fred so Sally could put in some lessons. Mark knocked on the door, Fred barked and this time, Sally thanked him in a cheery voice. Fred carried on barking, so Sally went to the door. Fred barked again whilst Sally was at the door, so she turned round, took him gently by the collar and isolated him. When Fred stopped barking, Sally let him out and we repeated the lesson. We did this several times, with Sally and Mark taking turns getting the door, until I saw evidence of them both perfecting the communication. After the consultation, they both seemed confident that they could tackle each element of Fred's behaviour.

Six months later, I got a call from Sally, claiming that Fred's behaviour had reverted, so we arranged to meet up again.

When I arrived, Sally informed me that she and Mark had split up. This had naturally affected Sally's mood. I requested that we put in some lessons so I could see what was going on. I asked Sally's next-door neighbour if she could knock on the door. Her neighbour knocked on the door and it was immediately clear that Sally had become less convincing in dealing with perceived danger; she was repeating herself with the acknowledgment of 'thank you' six times, and her tone was becoming progressively frustrated each time she spoke. She was then going towards the door, but was isolating Fred to stop him barking before she checked the perceived danger. As a result, Fred was no longer convinced of her leadership and there was a struggle for power.

I explained to Sally how her body language and tonality were painting a different picture than before. I reminded her to just say thank you once when Fred barked, but to be more jolly and calm with her tone. If he barked again, she should go straight to the door and put her hand on the handle so he knew she was checking the danger. She should then wait and, if he continued to bark, isolate him. We tried again, Sally thanked Fred in a cheery voice when he started barking and, this time, when she went to the door and put her hand on the handle, Fred settled. Sally looked surprised. I pointed out that if she had not gone right up to the door, he would have carried on barking because he didn't believe she was dealing with the perceived danger. Isolating him prematurely failed to display her intentions and her leadership – and saying thank you six times in an increasingly frustrated tone was not helping either. Sally explained she was a lot less patient since Mark left and told me she would make every effort to be more convincing.

Fred taught me a couple of lessons the second time I was there. Firstly, dogs can be unforgiving when their guardian's leadership subsides, no matter what the reason is. Secondly, it is vital that we use the right body language and tonality consistently to properly communicate the message to the dog. Any incongruence in our language or behaviour will be picked up by them.

I recall another case to highlight this, where the guardians were answering the intercom to see who their visitors were. The guardians at this point had to turn away from the door to answer the intercom. In this moment, the dog would no longer be convinced they were dealing with the danger and so carried on barking. As soon as the owner was conscious of how their body language looked to the dog, they corrected it by facing the door whilst talking on the intercom, and their dog instantly relaxed.

Fight

Aggression is an all too common problem in dogs, and is one of the most serious. A dog trying to control a situation can use aggression to see off the potential threat, especially if flight and freezing have not worked.

Dotty's story

A client called Susan asked if I could stay at her home to dog-sit and work with her Yorkshire Terrier, Dotty, whilst she was away on holiday. Susan was keen to rectify Dotty's behavioural problems, which consisted of pulling on the lead and barking at any dog she saw. If the dog came near Dotty, she would lunge and attack them.

I arrived at Susan's home and she suggested we go for a walk so she could show me the area where she lived and I could see Dotty's problematic behaviour. The three of us went out and Susan led me towards her local park through a long, narrow path. Dotty was clearly stressed with all the dogs that were on the path; she was pulling on the lead, barking and trying to attack them. Her attempts to deal with the situation appeared futile, as each time she reacted undesirably, Susan would jerk her back. This did not stop Dotty as, from her perspective, the behaviour was working – every dog was moving out of our way. Once we arrived at the park, Susan let Dotty off the lead and she immediately relaxed, ran around and sniffed the ground.

When we were walking back home on the narrow path, the situation went back to how it was before, with Dotty attempting to see off any other dog she saw. Once we returned home, Susan shortly left for her holiday.

A couple of hours later, I began teaching Dotty to heel in the home off lead and then on lead. Once that was accomplished, we went outside on a quiet street, where there were no dogs around, to carry on the lesson. Over the next few days, I continued to avoid dogs and teach Dotty to walk to heel, and she quickly learned that I was leading.

I then searched for areas where other dogs would be to demonstrate to Dotty that I would provide for her needs. The goal was to pass other dogs without Dotty barking. I found a suitable place where I also had the option to choose flight by walking away in different directions when I needed to. Soon, we saw a dog from roughly 50 metres away. I saw the first signal from Dotty that she was concerned, so I quickly reacted by walking away from the dog. However, I was too late and Dotty barked. At this moment, I walked away from the dog and said 'good girl' to Dotty in a jolly, reassuring tone.

This was the first time Dotty had experienced someone demonstrating that they were aware of the danger and would take her away from it. I will never forget the look on her face in that moment. It expressed absolute relief and curiosity, as if to say 'You understand me?' We walked off together in the opposite direction and she trotted along next to me. I looked for more dogs to put in more lessons. Each time we saw a dog about 50 metres away and I saw Dotty's state rising, I changed direction before it could heighten further. This action was interrupting her usual pattern of behaviour.

The next day, Dotty seemed relaxed with dogs from 50 metres away, so I took her closer. We got roughly 40 metres away from a dog and her state began to rise. In the low-level point of her state rising, I again walked off before she barked. I found many dogs and repeated these lessons many times at this distance. Over the following days, Dotty's state become increasing relaxed at this distance because she knew that I would deal with the perceived danger, so I closed the gap between us and other dogs. We went from 40 metres to 30, to 20 to ten, to five to two. There were times when Dotty would bark if I did not pick up on her state rising, but I would then thank her in a jolly tone and immediately react by walking away.

Now Dotty felt confident near dogs from a couple of metres away, I wanted her to socialise with them to see they were not a threat. If I saw a friendly-looking owner and a happy-looking dog, I would start up a conversation with them in an attempt to keep them there with Dotty positioned behind me (freeze). This was an opportunity to show Dotty that dogs were not a threat to her safety. I would ask the guardian if it was okay to stroke the dog. The guardian would say yes each time, so I would put my hand out. In this moment, Dotty would observe my body language, interacting with the dog using a friendly tone. This language communicated that I was okay with this. Dotty's state was calm so I allowed the dogs to meet for a bit. Dotty would sniff the other dog and walk away. We continued this with more dogs, each encounter boosting Dotty's confidence and belief that they were not a threat.

On a couple of these encounters, Dotty was uncertain of the other dogs we met. Her state heightened and she went to lunge and bark at them from behind me. I moved her back (roughly 10 metres) until her state reduced and then returned to the dog to carry on stroking it. By doing this, I was saying, 'I do not need you to deal with this, I am making the decisions.' I would then return to reinforce the lesson that this dog was okay.

On my last day with Dotty, we walked in the direction of the park on the narrow pavement that we'd first travelled with Susan. Dotty was calm with the other dogs walking past us. If they came too close, I would just move out of their way. These movements were enough to communicate that I was listening and still taking care of her. We got to the park and back home via the narrow path without her barking, lunging or pulling once.

The next day, Susan came home. I told her about the success I had with Dotty and we all went for a walk. Dotty was very calm and well-behaved the whole time. Susan was very pleased to see this. I explained to Susan how to adopt the role of guardian by understanding Dotty's needs and language and reacting to her concerns. Susan understood she had to communicate the role and was keen to relay the message to Dotty. I then left her to carry it on.

Dotty taught me how our motivations must be aligned with those of our dogs. Susan was doing what many well-intentioned guardians do, by taking her dog to the park twice a day for exercise. But Dotty was going out each day to warn other dogs away from her territory. As a result, Dotty felt she had to take control and negative patterns of behaviour had unknowingly formed.

It does not matter what your dog perceives as danger, be it certain dogs' breeds, people in wheelchairs, men with beards, people in uniform, animals on the television, the vacuum cleaner, etc. If we show our dogs we acknowledge their concern, no matter how trivial it appears to us, and react with flight or freeze – checking out the perceived danger (putting a consequence in if necessary) – it will demonstrate that we are listening to them and are making the decisions. Once they are calm enough to evaluate you in your role and the situation, it will boost their confidence and in turn, allow new patterns of behaviour to form.

Added tips

Inside

- Make sure you are between your dog and the perceived danger. To do that inside the home, you may have to claim your space by moving your dog back if it is trying to get past you.
- If your dog is concerned about loud noises such as fireworks or thunder and lightning etc. then thank them once, have a look, but then do nothing else. Your dog will assess your body language and tone and work out that you are not worried about the perceived danger. If they perceive you as leader, their confidence in the situation will grow over time.
- You can put on a performance to make the message clearer that you are taking care of dangers by patrolling boundaries such as the garden, making yourself bigger by puffing out your chest, raising your arms, and putting your hands on what they are concerned about.
- Having your dog on lead in many scenarios will assure you're able to keep your dog under control whilst communicating your role.
- Make sure your dog understands that you deal with dangers in the home before going out. This builds good foundations.

Outside

- Each outing should be geared towards accumulating experiences wherein you see, acknowledge and deal with the perceived danger before your dog. If you are successful, you can give yourself a tick for a positive leadership experience. If your dog deals with the danger (by attempting to flee, barking or lunging) before you do then give yourself a cross for a negative leadership experience. To make progress and clearly communicate that you are taking care of danger, each outing needs an overwhelming percentage of successful passes (ticks) to your dog thinking it is dealing with the danger (crosses).

- If your dog reacts in a panicked state, you are too close.

- The more stressed your dog is, the more calm and reactive you need to be.

- Plan the areas where you walk.

- Take it one step at a time and ensure each lesson is positive.

- If you feel there is a chance your dog may bite another person or dog, it is a necessary precaution to have your dog wearing a muzzle. Once the problem behaviour has been rectified, you can put the muzzle in the bin!

- Watch the video tutorial on my website.

Chapter 9
Dogs That Do Not Get On
With Each Other

There are some sad cases in which dogs that live together do not get on with each other. In the best-case scenarios, they tolerate but ignore one another; in the worst-case scenarios, they fight. If the guardian is perceived as leader, the squabbles in the pack are much less common and intense.

Zuma and Zoe's story

A client called K was distraught because his dogs – Zuma, a chocolate Labrador, and Zoe, a bulldog cross beagle – had suddenly started fighting with each other. The most recent incident had become so serious that both dogs needed medical attention.

K called me to his home for help. I was greeted by a number of people who worked for him in his home. My initial thought was that this was not going to be easy, as I needed each person who interacted with the dogs to keep up the communication for the messages to be consistent.

When I walked in, I saw both dogs were tied up at opposite ends of the room. K and his assistants were all worried something was going to happen at any minute. I could feel the tense atmosphere. K told me about the issues and I explained why the fighting was happening, because the dogs were competing for the leadership role, but if they understood their place in the pack, they would not fight. I then talked the humans through the Guardian Role principles and how to address the situation. Once K and his assistants knew what to do, I left and asked them to keep me informed of how they got on.

They all immediately began communicating their role and addressing the situation. They took precautions for the dogs' safety by walking them separately and feeding them in different rooms. The dogs were rarely left alone in the room together and, if they were, they were tied up so they could not get at each other.

Over the following days, the dogs became more relaxed. If Zuma or Zoe growled or showed any signs of aggression towards one another, they were put into isolation to calm down. Quickly, the dogs realised that any signs of aggression would mean being removed from the pack.

Each day that went by, one of the assistants informed me of signs of progress. Inside the home, the dogs were using playful gestures from across the room, such as a play bow combined with a tail wag. The assistants picked up on their happy state and closed the gap to see their reaction. If they appeared fine, they were allowed to get closer to one another and interact in a controlled manner for a short time to ensure the experience was positive. The dogs were now being walked together outside, a few metres apart, and appeared fine.

The assistants progressed by taking the dogs out for a walk side by side. Once they returned home, the dogs would display more friendly gestures to one another, and so were permitted to interact with each other off lead.

If play ever became too rough, K or one of the assistants would come in and split them up before their state could heighten by moving them away or isolating them. They only had to do this a couple of times until the dogs understood the rules of how to play nicely. Now that Zoe and Zuma were free from responsibility and the stress of who was the leader, they were back to being the best of friends.

Chapter 10
Attention-Seeking
Behaviours

Many dogs seek to gain human attention, and manage this by displaying a range of behaviours including whining, barking, stealing objects, bringing toys, pawing, nudging, jumping up, and leaning or sitting on the person in question. This behaviour is often interpreted as excitement, wanting a cuddle or to play, a sign that the dog has missed you, is bored, and so on. Any of these explanations may carry some truth as dogs do have a need for company, affection and stimulation and so will search for these things. However, if a dog believes it is able to manoeuvre humans, it will soon receive the wrong information about its role within the group dynamic. It is therefore vital that you are in control of when your dog's needs for interaction and play are fulfilled and not the other way around.

Invading people's space

Danny's story

Pamela and David were the guardians to a Golden Retriever named Danny. Danny would regularly invade their personal space each time they entered the home and many times throughout the day. He would also jump on Pamela and David's guests inside the home and on strangers when out on a walk. If any person were to give Danny a stroke, he would love the attention and sit down. But the moment they stopped, he would jump on them in a bid to get more attention. He was a big, strong dog, which made his intrusive behaviour difficult to control. Pamela and David were going away for a much-needed holiday and they asked if I could stay at their home and work on Danny's issues in their absence.

When I first arrived at Pamela and David's home, I withheld greeting Danny in order to send the message that, as leader, I would decide when it was time to interact (the golden five-minute ritual). Danny ignored this message and attempted to get my attention by pushing his muzzle into my hands. Once he saw I was not reacting to him, he jumped up at me. I continued to withhold greeting him whilst simultaneously showing him his intrusive behaviour was not welcome by pushing him away. This action seemed to make him worse; he came back and jumped up on me with more force as if to say, 'Who do you think you are, pushing me away?' I reacted by asking Pamela to take him by the collar and isolate him in the nearest room. After 10 seconds, I let him out of isolation. Immediately, he came bounding back and jumped on me again. So I asked Pamela to isolate him again, but this time, I left him there for 20 seconds before letting him out. Once out, he again ran back and persisted in invading my space.

Pamela kept isolating him each time he invaded my space – for a little longer each time – and letting him back out to give him the opportunity to learn from his mistakes. However, Danny was extremely strong-willed and the golden five-minute ritual became over an hour with no sign of him giving up. New attention-seeking tactics of chasing his tail were also in evidence. As a result, I instructed Pamela to take him by the collar and use the calm freeze until he stopped the undesirable behaviour. Finally, after an hour and a quarter, Danny gave up and left me alone. Shortly afterwards, Pamela and David left to go on their holiday.

It was clear from the tenacity of Danny's attention-seeking behaviour that he was going to be a challenging case. In response, I identified and planned to address his behaviour in stages. This ensured that I had a clear focus of where to start and the necessary steps to reach the end goal.

To begin with, I planned to teach him to respect my space each time I walked through the door. It had taken an hour and a quarter for him to leave me alone the first time we were introduced, so I aimed to improve on that by walking in and out of the front door many times, adopting the golden five-minute ritual. If he jumped up at me at any point, I would move him away; if he persisted, I would isolate him. I kept doing this until I was free to walk in and out of the home without being accosted. I also ensured that I withheld from interacting with him if he came up to me throughout the day.

Stage two was to teach him not to jump up at me after I stopped stroking him. To address this, I would call him over for attention and Danny would run over very excitedly, enjoying the interaction. As soon as I stopped stroking him, I would turn away, demonstrating clearly that the attention had finished. Danny, however, jumped on me again to ask for more attention and so I isolated him. I kept repeating this process – calling him over and cuddling him, but then stopping so he could learn when the attention started and stopped.

Meanwhile, each time we went for a walk, I avoided passing other people so Danny couldn't jump on them. I would stick to the quiet streets and cross the road each time I saw somebody. He was desperate to go over to people; he would pull on the lead and stand up on his hind legs in his attempts.

In response, I would use the calm freeze until he relaxed and then, once he was calm, I would release the collar and walk on. After doing this a few times with different people, Danny became frustrated at not being able to approach them and upped his game with a new behaviour of spinning in circles, making it very hard to hold onto him. In fact, I had to use all my energy to keep him there. Eventually, after a minute of holding on, he would calm down and stop, so I would release my grip on his collar and we would walk on. This became a common theme: if he saw a dog or a person that he wanted to interact with, he would attempt with all his strength to get to them. And each time, I would use the calm freeze to teach him it was not his choice whom he could go up and say hello to.

Stage three was to teach him to respect my personal space when I was sitting on the floor. I would instigate many lessons by sitting on the floor throughout the day but would not look at him, thus sending the message that I did not want to interact. Danny could not resist jumping on me when I was on the floor, so I would move him away and isolate him as many times as needed until I could sit on the floor without him invading my space. I would then mix the lessons up by sitting on the floor and calling him over for a stroke and then stopping. When Danny stopped jumping up on me after I gave him a big cuddle whilst sitting on the floor, it felt like a major breakthrough. My hope was that this respect of personal space would translate to Pamela, David, their visitors and people outside.

Stage four was teaching him not to jump up at visitors when they came into the home. Pamela had put me in touch with friends who were willing to come and help with the teaching. They knew to go through the golden five-minute ritual each time they saw Danny. Once they came in, Danny would pester them. They would withhold greeting Danny, as instructed, until he left them alone. If he became a nuisance, I moved him away or isolated him until he had learnt the lesson. Once Danny left them alone, I would ask our visitors to call him over and give him attention. They stroked him but, once they stopped, he showed self-restraint and did not bother them further. A positive result!

As the days went past, Danny demonstrated that he was able to listen to me on the walk and pay less attention to other people. So I took it a stage further by going up to people and starting a conversation. I explained what I was doing with Danny and asked if they would interact with him by calling them over into their space. They all kindly agreed to call him over and give him a stroke. I was ready to use a calm freeze if he jumped up on the person, but he behaved impeccably.

When Pamela and David returned, Danny was very pleased to see them but he did not invade their space. I explained how the week had gone and what they should do in each scenario. Since then, they have followed the advice to the letter. They still have their extremely affectionate dog who is excited to see people, but now he understands not to enter their space unless invited. As a result, he gets more cuddles now than ever before.

Added tips

- Even if your dog is small, do not let them invade your space unless invited.
- Don't forget: the golden five-minute ritual does not necessarily take five minutes. It takes as long as is necessary for your dog to leave you alone.
- Remember, you still must fulfil your dog's needs by giving them lots of attention, cuddles and play; but to facilitate your role, it just has to be on your terms.
- Watch the video tutorial on my website.

Stealing objects

Daphne and Daisy's story

Laura was the mother to a young girl named Belle and guardian to two Weimaraners named Daphne and Daisy. Daphne and Daisy would regularly take Belle's toys and chew them. They also stole balls from other dogs playing in the park and Laura would struggle to get them back and returned to the rightful owners. Laura had decided enough was enough and called me in for help.

Once I arrived at the home, Daphne and Daisy grabbed their toys and paraded around the front room with them in their mouths. Once they realised they were not getting my attention, they proceeded to pull the cushions off the couch and brought them to me. I asked Laura to calmly retrieve the cushions without speaking to them. Laura managed to take the cushions away and put them back on the couch. Daphne returned to grab the cushion again, so I asked Laura to repeat the process and then isolate her as a consequence of her action. I instructed Laura to repeat this consequence each time the dogs took something that was not theirs. This carried on for some time, with both dogs picking up many different objects in the home, from shoes to bags to Belle's toys until, finally, they both resisted picking anything up and settled down.

Laura proceeded to tell me about the problems she was encountering with Daphne and Daisy stealing other dogs' balls when out for a walk. Whilst Laura was talking, I noticed she was reaching over to the dogs to pet them and speak to them many times. I lost count of how many times she did this, but it was over fifty within a one-hour period. I mentioned to Laura that by constantly looking at, touching and speaking to her dogs, she was communicating the message that she needed them. I added that this was a main factor as to why they were displaying manic behaviour, namely because she was unknowingly communicating to Daphne and Daisy that they were the ones in charge.

Laura admitted she was missing Belle in the daytimes and so was often talking to and making more of a fuss of her dogs. I responded by explaining that she could still cuddle and play with them as much as she wanted; it just had to be on her terms. Laura claimed that if she called them over, they would often not come to her. I pointed out that if they didn't come over, it was probably because they were challenging her and testing the boundaries, or perhaps because they simply didn't want a cuddle and that decision had to be respected.

Quite simply, if a guardian constantly calls their dog over without there being anything in it for the dog, it will resist.

Once the consultation had finished, Laura understood she had to change her own behaviours in order to address the issues and immediately started communicating her role as guardian. In the following days, she stopped going up to the dogs, and only communicated with them on her terms, which was a lot less often than before. With each day that went by, the dogs got into the habit of coming over when Laura called them. She also set aside time to play with them each day and made sure she was the one instigating this. Each time the dogs grabbed something that was not theirs, Laura removed it, and if they persisted, they were isolated. There were many days when Daphne and Daisy were particularly demanding and attempted to get Laura's attention by dropping their toys in her lap. In response, she would pick the toys up and put them away.

Laura began taking each dog out separately and on a long lead in order to teach them not to steal balls from other people or dogs. She would actively seek out people and dogs playing with balls and walk close to them. If either Daphne or Daisy went to go for the ball, she would interrupt their pattern of behaviour by taking the dog by the collar, moving her back until she had their attention and then returning to walk near the dog playing with the ball. This was repeated again and again until each dog resisted stealing any ball, no matter how close they were to it. Once the dogs stopped their negative behaviour whilst on a long lead, Laura progressed to letting them back off lead. In this scenario, they were still well-behaved, so finally, she took them out together again. Daphne and Daisy behaved well in their new-found freedom and were responsive to Laura's instructions. Laura was delighted.

A few months later, however, I got a call from Laura telling me she had experienced a setback and that Daphne and Daisy had reverted to old behaviours. I asked her a number of questions in order to ascertain why she thought that was. After chatting for a while, Laura admitted she was going up to the dogs again. I asked her why she was doing that, to which she responded that as the dogs had been behaving so well, she thought it would be okay to do so. I reiterated to Laura the following crucial point: dogs will always assess your language and, if you are seen to be acting in a subordinate manner, they will assume the role of leader again. I pointed out that communication is for life, not just a few months. Consequently, Laura immediately went back to communicating her role and quickly got back on track.

Added tips

- If your dog is ball-obsessed, you can work on the foundations in the home by playing with a ball with another family member. If the dog goes for the ball whilst you are playing with it then isolate them. Then let them out and repeat the lesson until they understand that, as leader, you will invite them when it is time to play.

Chapter 11
Rough Play

When your dog plays too roughly with another dog, it is necessary to intervene. You will likely encounter some guardians who question your actions and proclaim the play as harmless. However, by not intervening, you are permitting your dog to have bad manners. If your dog develops bad manners, sooner or later, another dog will have to tell it off and this can quickly escalate into a fight. To avoid any incidents, teach your dog to be calm and respectful whilst playing with other dogs.

Milo's story

Rupert was the guardian to a Rhodesian Ridgeback crossbreed called Milo. Rupert called me to explain that Milo had recently been getting into a number of fights with other dogs and asked me to come to his home to help make sense of the situation.

Once I arrived, Milo immediately attempted to get my attention by invading my space and jumping up. I explained to Rupert how to correct Milo's behaviour and Rupert intervened.

After a few lessons, Milo left me alone. As Rupert began telling me about the fights Milo had been involved in, Milo got up on the couch and sat on Rupert's lap. I pointed out to Rupert that Milo was not respecting his personal space. Rupert said he didn't mind and quite liked it. I explained that if Milo did not respect his guardian's personal space, he was less likely to respect that of visitors or other dogs. Rupert then mentioned that Milo went up to many dogs, but claimed that he was just being friendly. I pointed out that he might have friendly intentions but if other dogs felt their space was being invaded, they would tell Milo off, and this could be the reason why the fights had started. Rupert added that Milo also played roughly with other dogs and agreed that he would address his behaviour to avoid any further problems.

I explained the Guardian Role principles to Rupert. After the consultation had finished, he was keen to get started and work on Milo's intrusive behaviour.

Rupert began in the home by correcting Milo each time his personal space was invaded. Quickly, Milo learnt the rules of who instigates attention in the home. When out on the walk, Rupert had Milo on a short lead in order to retain control of Milo when meeting dogs. If Milo became too excited and attempted to go up to another dog, Rupert would walk him in the opposite direction, thus demonstrating that he was the one deciding where to go and whom to greet. This was repeated many times until Milo was responsive to Rupert's decisions. Now that Milo was behaving on lead near dogs, Rupert experimented by greeting a guardian and their dog. The moment Milo became too boisterous and invaded the dog's space, Rupert would interrupt his behaviour by taking him by the collar and walking him away. Once he calmed, Rupert would take him back to the situation. This was repeated many times and with many dogs until Milo was calm and respectful on a short lead in other dogs' company.

The next stage was to give Milo a bit more freedom by having him on a long lead. This gave Rupert the necessary control to intervene if Milo's behaviour needed correcting. Milo would go up to other dogs and draw them into a game. If he played nicely, Rupert left him to it. If he became overexcited and played roughly, Rupert intervened the same way, by taking him by the collar and walking him away, therefore giving him a chance to calm and reflect on his actions before returning.

Once Milo was respecting other dogs' personal space on a long lead, Rupert finally let him off lead and was prepared to intervene if needed. Rupert reported to me that he only had to intervene a couple more times and now Milo is playing nicely with other dogs. More importantly, he is not getting into any more fights!

Added tips

- Teach your dog manners in the home.
- Socialise your dog by having it interact with well-mannered, calm dogs. This way, your dog will learn the rules of play. If your dog becomes intrusive in the other dog's space, intervene.

Chapter 12
Separation Anxiety

Separation anxiety can occur in dogs due to a combination of unmet needs. Some dogs may feel they are leader and are therefore responsible for their guardian's safety. Once the guardian leaves, the dog panics because it can no longer protect the guardian. Dogs do not understand where we have gone or if we will ever return. Other dogs, usually puppies, may not think they are in charge of the guardian, but they feel unsafe once the guardian leaves, lacking confidence that they will ever return. The stress that occurs from separation anxiety manifests itself in a range of behaviours such as constantly following the guardians in the home, barking/howling/whining when they leave, scratching the door, not settling, chewing objects, toileting in the house and much more.

The good news is, whatever the reason for the separation anxiety, it can be resolved in the same way: demonstrating that you provide for all their needs whilst boosting their confidence that when you leave, you will come back.

Badger's story

Badger, a rescue Staffordshire bull terrier belonging to Marcy and Guy, had a severe case of separation anxiety. He was absolutely fine with Marcy leaving the home, but when Guy left, he instantly became distraught. He would whine and bark until Guy returned. This happened even if Marcy was still in the flat. Badger's barking was a huge problem for Guy as he lived in a block of flats and he was concerned not only for the wellbeing of the other residents, but also for Badger.

I arrived at Guy's home. He told me he had tried some techniques to stop Badger's behaviour, such as ensuring he did not communicate with him when he came in and when he left. He also told me he was leaving objects such as Kongs containing food as a distraction. But nothing had worked.

I explained the Guardian Role principles. I acknowledged that, although Guy was doing some things right – such as walking in and out without acknowledging Badger – the other factors were not in place, and this was confusing Badger as to who the real leader was.

I asked Guy to walk in and out of the flat so I could see how Badger reacted. Guy got off the couch and Badger followed. As soon as Guy walked out of the front door, Badger became stressed and started barking. Guy then came back into the flat and sat down.

I explained to Guy how heightened Badger's state was and that it was very traumatic for him. To address his behaviour, we had to desensitise him to the triggers that made him panic. The goal was for Badger not to worry when Guy left the flat. As Badger was following him as soon as he got off the couch, the first thing we had to accomplish was for Guy to get off the couch without Badger reacting. So I instructed Guy to get up, walk one metre away and return without looking at or speaking to Badger. As soon as Guy got up, Badger followed. Guy walked a metre before coming back to sit on the couch. Badger was now up and paused for a minute, looking confused before lying back down. Once Badger had settled, I got Guy to repeat the process many times until Badger eventually decided not to bother getting up at all. This meant that Badger had become desensitised to Guy getting off the couch and so his state was no longer rising to panic. It was small progress, but it gave us something to build on.

The next checkpoint was for Guy to get up, walk three metres and come back again. Initially, as soon as Guy walked past a metre, Badger followed him. So the lesson was repeated again and again until Guy could get off the couch, walk three metres and return without Badger getting up.

Now came the time for Guy to take things further by going up to his shoes, which were next to the front door. This involved Guy passing the three-metre boundary and resulted in Badger leaping up. Guy responded by returning to the living room and sitting back down again. As with the previous stages, Guy repeated this action until it was clear that Badger was able to stay relaxed enough not to follow him. Once the consultation had finished, Guy felt confident he knew what he had to do.

Guy was fortunate to work from home so had lots of opportunities to put lessons into practice for Badger. Over the following days, he identified the triggers to Badger's heightening state and took the steps to actively desensitise them. He would get up off the couch to put his shoes on then take them off and sit back down again. He would put his coat on, take it off and come back. Eventually, he successfully built up to putting his shoes and coat on and going out the door for one second.

The next stage was to extend the time he remained outside the door from one second to five seconds, to ten, to twenty, and then up to several minutes. Badger would occasionally follow but, in response, Guy would reduce the time or distance and then slowly build it back up again.

It took time and patience. Upon speaking to Guy weeks later, he said he had experienced a few setbacks when he had become lax with the other necessary parts of the communication process, which reminded him how important it was to consistently communicate to Badger that he was leading in ALL areas.

More often than not with separation anxiety, leaving the dog can be done in stages – i.e. for five seconds before coming back in again, then ten seconds and so on. But as Badger's case was so extreme, it was necessary to reduce the goal to something we could achieve, making sure he was comfortable with checkpoints and building it up slowly to stages.

Added tips

- Remember not to interact with your dog by saying goodbye when you leave the home. It will likely confuse it.
- Life is often not perfect; sometimes, you will have to go out and leave your dog on its own. In this scenario, you can manage the home by picking up your belongings and sellotaping cardboard on the door to stop your dog damaging it.
- Start off getting your dog used to you moving around the home without them following you before going outside.

Chapter 13
The Walk – On Lead

One of the most common problems people experience with their dogs is out on the walk. Dogs can pull on the lead, chew the lead, twist in circles, run off, freeze or even refuse to go on the walk in the first place.

Freezing on the walk

Ted's story

One of the most memorable dog-sitting experiences I encountered was with a large crossbreed called Ted. His guardians, Kris and Michael, asked me to stay in their home and look after Ted while they went away for a few weeks. I was there purely to look after Ted, rather than address his behaviour, as he appeared to be a very calm, relaxed dog. However, despite this, Ted taught me an invaluable lesson in communication.

I came to Kris and Michael's home the morning they were leaving for their holiday. They told me Ted's routine and showed me around the house. Shortly after they left, Ted and I began bonding.

I took him out for a walk to the local park, which had many different routes around it. I chose one and began to walk. But Ted pulled back on the lead, sat down and would not move forward.

I gave the lead a gentle tug and encouraged him to come but he refused to budge. I looked around to see why he had stopped. There wasn't anything around that could be perceived to cause him harm – no other dogs, no people, no airplanes flying overhead. I could not drag him, as that would have compromised our friendship, so after a minute, I changed direction to walk another route. This time, Ted happily followed.

The next day, we went back to the park. I chose to walk down the same route that had made him freeze the previous day to see if he would do the same thing. We arrived at the lane and once again, Ted froze in the same spot. I had another look around for anything that could be perceived as danger but, as with the previous day, there did not appear to be anything. Again, I gave the lead a little tug but Ted refused to budge. At this point, it was important to make clear that he could not dictate which direction we took, so I turned my back to him to communicate that I made the decisions and this was the way we were going. I figured he would eventually get bored, give in and follow me. But 10 minutes later, he had not moved and I was the one getting bored! So I must admit that I gave in and went back in the direction that Ted wanted to go.

For the duration of my stay, I could have easily avoided going down the particular route Ted froze at, but his behaviour had become a challenge that I wanted to understand and overcome. I devised a plan to get him to follow me down the route in question. The next time I tried to get him to take it and he refused, I would use a treat to encourage him to follow me, drop the lead and walk down the path (calling him once and then walking away). This, I reasoned, would deal with any resistance and ensure he saw me as the leader and the one who made the decisions.

The next day, I went with Ted to the park, ready to carry out this plan. Sure enough, as soon as we got to the same spot, Ted froze. So I dropped the lead, called him once while showing him a treat and walked off down the path.

After 20 seconds, I looked back only to see him rooted to the same spot. I went around the corner out of his sight and peered round to watch his reaction but he just sat there, waiting. After a minute, I became concerned he would move off in the opposite direction so I returned and, once again, we ended up going in the direction Ted wanted to go.

I was disheartened and frustrated. What was I missing? I had established all the foundations of leadership; he saw me gesture eat; he did not bark when people came to the door; he did not invade my space; I completed the golden five-minute ritual after each separation, interacted with him on my terms and he walked to heel. Everything was going very well – except for this one thing.

At a loss, I decided to go back to the beginning and practise walking in the home. I called Ted over to me and we did some stop/start/change direction off lead, with treats. Ted happily followed me, so after a few minutes, I put him on the lead and did the same thing. After 30 seconds, Ted froze and would not budge, exactly like in the park. I was dumbfounded. Why was he now challenging me in the home? It was as if his behaviour was regressing. I figured that at least in the home, I could control the situation, so I took the lead off and abandoned going on the afternoon walk. This way, I was able to take his decision-making away in an environment where I had control without the fear of him walking away.

A few hours went by, giving me time to ponder the situation. I eventually realised this could be turned to my advantage: if Ted was freezing in the home then we simply would not go outside until he followed me where I decided to go. I called him over and did some more stop/start/change direction. This time, Ted followed me for a minute before he froze. I immediately took the lead off him, thus communicating that I had abandoned going on the walk.

The next morning, I tried again. This time, Ted followed me for a few minutes before he decided to freeze. This was a considerable improvement on the previous day. I again took the lead off and realised I was making progress. After several attempts of calling him over, changing direction and abandoning the walk each time he froze, we were eventually walking around the house for a long time without Ted freezing. I then walked out the front door to the park and headed straight for the route where it had all begun. This time, Ted walked with me and without any resistance.

It dawned on me that Ted had not previously seen me as the decision-maker on the walk. While walking to the park with him, I thought I was showing that I was making the decisions of when to go, where to go and at what speed, but Ted must have thought he was making those decisions. It only became apparent when we disagreed on where to go, and I had made it worse by giving in to him when he protested. It just so happened that we had walked to the park without any problems, but only because we were heading where he wanted to go and at a pace he chose!

Most other dogs that believe they are leading the walk will display more obvious signs, especially if they are scared or lack confidence when outside. They will typically pull on the lead whilst panting heavily, some will be in such a heightened state, their eyes will bulge, whilst others will move from one side of the pavement to the other. Ted was a rare case. He had bags of confidence in his surroundings, he did not fear anything, but he thought he was telling me where he wanted to go.

Ted taught me the value of never assuming I am the leader. Since then, I rigidly stick to the stages on the walk and change speed, practise manoeuvres and turn to see if they accept that I am leading or resist. I then moderate my lessons accordingly.

Pulling on the lead

Renzo's story

Christine and Simon had a rescue Rottweiler called Renzo. Renzo was very calm and well-behaved in the home but as soon as he got outside, his state heightened and he pulled on the lead. As Renzo was a large dog, his pulling made walks an unpleasant experience for all involved. Christine and Simon had to visit relatives abroad and so asked me to stay in their home in order to work on Renzo's behaviour.

I began by teaching Renzo to walk to heel in the home and garden. Once I was sure he would follow me without any problems, we ventured outside onto a quiet street to continue the lesson. As soon as we walked out the front door, he began pulling on the lead. I corrected each of his pulls by stopping, starting and then continuing or changing direction. Renzo pulled on the lead many times, and I corrected him every time. By the end of the day, I felt I had made progress on his pulling, but when we went out the next day, it was as if he had forgotten it all and we had to start all over again.

After a week of going out on walks with Renzo on the quiet street and correcting his pulls, it did not seem that I was making any significant progress. He was still pulling.

Christine and Simon were due home in a few days and I became frustrated with the speed of Renzo's progress. But the more frustrated and stressed I became, the more Renzo would pull, even harder than before. I realised that I had to stay calm in order to get back on track, but I was finding it extremely hard to hide my feelings.

With only two days until Christine and Simon returned, I got up early to take Renzo out for an extra lesson. After just a few metres, Renzo once again pulled on the lead. I became instantly frustrated and took him by the collar and walked him back into the home. I went into the kitchen on my own to try and calm myself so he wouldn't see my frustration, as I did not want any more setbacks. I regained my composure and we went back out again. This time, Renzo did not pull for about 20 metres, which was the furthest we had ever got without any problems. As soon as he pulled, I again took him by the collar, walked him back into the house and went into the kitchen, as I wanted to see if it was doing this that had caused him to walk so far without pulling. Ten minutes later, we went out again. This time, Renzo did not pull for 50 metres. And again, as soon as he did pull, I took him by the collar and led him back into the house. I kept repeating this for the following two days, and by the end of it, we were walking for 20 minutes without a pull. Wherever we were, however far we'd got, if he pulled, I would take him by the collar and come home.

I realised that, in Renzo's case, the tactics of praising, feeding, rewarding or walking back a few metres did not have the desired effect as it did nothing to calm his state. But taking him home when he pulled and leaving him on his own gave him time to calm down and reflect on his actions. Christine and Simon came home to a reformed dog.

Added tips

- Make sure there is no tension in the lead, otherwise you will be controlling the dog. The lead must be loose to allow the dog to pull so you can correct it.
- If your dog freezes because it is nervous, you have to be extra patient and rigidly stick to the stages.
- Don't become frustrated when your dog pulls – each time you correct your dog with a lesson, it means you are one step closer.
- Allow time and remain calm.
- If necessary, think about how you can create checkpoints at each stage. For example, if your dog walks to heel in the home but is in a heightened state when it gets outside, try teaching it to heel in the home (on lead) with the front door open and then move forward once it is calm.
- Ensure that no one is undoing your work by not following these rules when they walk your dog for you.
- Watch the video tutorial on my website.

Chapter 14
The Walk – Off Lead

If your dog perceives you as leader but just needs teaching the correct response of coming to you when you call them, the 'off-lead advice' of 'call once then leave' in Chapter 4 will suffice. However, if your dog is particularly challenging in this area, an effective way to address the issue is by teaching your dog the recall response on a long lead in stages. This will give you the necessary control to communicate that you are making the decisions about where to go on the walk, whilst avoiding any mishaps.

Recall in stages

To begin with, make sure you have strong leadership foundations before moving forward: your dog understands that you are entitled to priority feeding and you will take care of dangers, you decide when to interact, and you lead the walk on lead, etc. Once these foundations are in place, practise the recall response in the home. To do this, look at your dog and call it to you in a friendly tone; if it comes to you, reward it with a treat and/or praise it. If the dog doesn't come, don't worry, as it has nowhere to go. Keep practising until the dog is responsive to your request. Then you can progress a stage forward by going to an environment with minimal distractions, such as a quiet area with grass.

Have your dog on a long lead and a harness. The latter is necessary so your dog does not injure itself by running at high speed and then jerking its neck. Practise the recall response, the same as in the home, by calling your dog to you; if it comes back, reward it with a treat and/or praise it. If it does not respond, however, gently but firmly bring it back to your side with the lead to show it what you are asking. Do not reward or praise it in this scenario. It is advisable to correct it outside as if it does not respond, it could find itself in a potentially dangerous situation. Keep repeating the lesson many times. Your dog will likely work out that if it comes of its own free will, it will get praise and/or a treat, and if it doesn't, you will correct it by bringing it back, so it may as well return.

If at any point your dog pulls at the end of the long lead in an effort to take you in a direction it chooses then (following the same principles as with the short lead) stop, start (bring it back to your side) and change direction.

When your dog understands not to pull on a long lead and is responding to your requests, a next stage would be to seek out an environment that will potentially contain distractions such as other people, children, another dog, or people having picnics, playing ball games etc. Start off with your chosen distraction far away in the distance so that your dog's state is below a 3 on the scale. Call your dog to you to see if it is being responsive; if it returns, reward and/or praise and then close the gap between your dog and the distraction. If it doesn't listen and is focused on the distraction, it means you are probably starting off too close, so bring your dog back to you and move further away again until you have its attention. Once it is listening, practise the response and move closer if it co-operates. If your dog stops responding at any point, more lessons are needed at that particular distance.

Once you get close to the distraction – let's say it is another dog – and you are happy for them to play (assuming the other dog appears friendly and wants to play, and the guardian is happy about it), then let it happen for a while and then practise the recall request. If your dog comes back, reward it and instantly let it play again so it sees the whole experience as positive. If it doesn't come back then a correction will be necessary: bring your dog to you to interrupt its state and take it away from the situation until it is calm and focused. Once you have its focus again, keep repeating the lesson until you have the desired response.

When your dog is coming to you each time you call it on a long lead, no matter what distractions or potential dangers it is faced with, you are in a position to let it off lead. However, if you are still concerned, to play it safe, you could add another stage, either by practising in a park with a fence surrounding it or, if you do not live near a park such as this, having your dog on a long lead that drags on the floor. This gives your dog more freedom whilst you still have control of the situation.

Once in this scenario, practise recall by calling your dog once, making sure it can hear you. If it doesn't come straight away, walk in the other direction; it will see you walking off and will probably follow you. If not, it will be necessary to go back to the stage at which your dog was listening on a long lead and progress from there.

Jasper's story

Jasper, the Parson Terrier, initially appeared to be an extremely hard case to address, not only because he displayed a multitude of problems, including running off and pulling on the lead, but also due to the extra complication of him being deaf. His owners, Sue and Graham, asked me to stay at their house to work on Jasper's behavioural problems whilst they went on holiday. When I met Sue, she suggested we take

Jasper for a walk to the park so she could show me the local area and I could witness Jasper's behaviour.

As soon as we walked out the door, Jasper's state heightened and he began pulling Sue in the direction of the park. Once there, Sue let him off the lead and he began to run at great speed in the direction of a car, which was driving through the park. It was pointless shouting his name as, because of Jasper's deafness, he would not be able to hear us; instead, Sue ran after him and, after some time, managed to get him back, luckily without incident. We went back home and shortly afterwards, Sue and Graham left for their holiday.

I was aware that I would have to communicate with Jasper using solely my body language. I started communicating my role to him in silence. If he barked at dangers in the home, I would get up and position myself in front of him and check them out. I would ask him to come to me by using a hand signal, rewarding him each time he responded correctly. I practised this hand signal over longer distances in the home so he got into the habit of looking to me. When out for walks, I would correct him each time he pulled and would wait for his state to calm before moving on. By the fourth day, Jasper walked to the park in a calm state, with only a few corrections required.

Once in the park, I put him on a long lead and began changing direction and speed to show him I was making the decisions of where to go and at what speed. I would signal for him to come to me many times on each walk and put in a reward or bring him to me, depending on his response. I would walk past potential dangers such as ponds, the road where cars would occasionally drive through, and the exits, to gauge his reaction. If he pulled on the long lead or would not respond to my hand gesture, I would correct him by bringing him back.

In the last days, Jasper's behaviour had significantly improved and he had learnt to look to me for guidance on his environment. Once the week was over, Sue and Graham came back and were pleasantly surprised to see their dog walk to the park without a pull and then demonstrate responsive behaviour on a long lead. After I relayed the communication, they carried on the work and, over time, they built up to letting Jasper off lead.

Despite Jasper being deaf, he was surprisingly easy to communicate with. Perhaps due to his hearing issues, he was even more desperate for leadership than an average dog. Once he was communicated to in a language he understood, he quickly handed over the role. Now Sue and Graham have a very happy, relaxed dog that looks to them for guidance. As a result, he does not attempt to lead the walk anymore.

Added tips

- There is no rush to let your dog off lead – its safety is more important.
- If you use a retractable lead, take extra caution.
- If your dog freezes when you're correcting it, focus primarily on encouraging them back with treats and praise.
- Never punish your dog when it returns; it will not associate the action with the consequence.
- Go out with a friend who has a dog with excellent recall in order to speed up the process.

Chapter 15
Obsessive Behaviours

Some dogs who become overwhelmed with the responsibility of believing they are leader demonstrate that they cannot cope by exhibiting a range of obsessive behaviours; these include chasing their tails, attacking light reflections on the wall, and self-mutilation, such as chewing their paws, pulling out their fur and much more.

Lucy's story

Madeline and John were the guardians to Lucy, a Dalmatian with obsessive behaviours, who would attack light reflections on the walls of their home. When Madeline and John took her to the park, she would pick up a stick, hold it in her mouth, and lie down; then her eyes would glaze over and she wouldn't let go of the stick. When this behaviour first developed, Madeline and John thought that it was playful and she would eventually grow out of it. However, over time, the behaviour only got worse and it became clear to them that Lucy was incredibly stressed.

Madeline and John explained on the phone that they had tried everything to stop her behaviour, from shouting and screaming at her, to distracting her with food and toys, to reassuring her, yet nothing had worked. They asked if I had ever before come across a dog exhibiting this sort of obsessive behaviour with a stick. Although I hadn't, I was optimistic that I could address the obsessive behaviour in the same way that all obsessive behaviour can be addressed – by communicating leadership, combined with interrupting the dog's heightened states and undesirable patterns of behaviour in order to create new, desirable patterns of behaviour.

When I arrived, Madeline and John invited me into their home and Lucy began pacing up and down. She grabbed her toys and brought them to me, and when that didn't succeed in getting my attention, she jumped up on me. I withheld greeting her until she left me alone. Madeline and John explained the problems they were having with Lucy in more detail and I gave them advice on how to apply the Guardian Role principles. After the consultation had finished, I left and Madeline and John immediately started to communicate their role.

Every time Lucy would attack light reflecting on the walls, either John or Madeline would take her by the collar without speaking, hold her close to their body (calm freeze) and turn her away from the light until her state lowered, and then release her. If she went back to attacking the light, they would repeat the process until she stopped. There were times where Lucy's state was severely heightened, so they would put her in another room to interrupt the pattern altogether. Once she was calm, they would let her out. They kept repeating this process until Lucy finally gave up, ignored the light flickering on the walls and relaxed.

Madeline and John acknowledged that Lucy wasn't obsessive with a stick in the house, but only in the park. This gave them the opportunity to assess the point when her state began to heighten and then develop into obsessive behaviour, and to interrupt it. When it was time for a walk, they began observing her state: it heightened when they walked out the door, so John would bring her back and wait for her to calm. Only then would they walk on. In the calm moments, Madeline would walk up with a stick and show it to Lucy. When Lucy was calm, she was not overly interested in it. However, as they got closer to the park, they could see Lucy's state rising dramatically so they would stop and go back again until she calmed. They kept repeating this, returning home if her state stayed at a high level. For many days, they got close to the park but didn't go in as a result of her heightened state. Once they were finally able to enter the park whilst she was in a calm state, Lucy did show interest in the stick but was relaxed enough to drop it when asked.

Lucy was not able to think rationally when in a heightened state, much like human beings. Our behaviour can also become erratic and our heightened state manifests itself in all sorts of ways, including anxiety, aggression, fear, avoidance, etc. John and Madeline were able to successfully judge Lucy's state and react appropriately each time to keep it down. This way, Lucy would always be coherent and would not exhibit any undesirable behaviour.

Added tips

- React quickly and don't make a fuss.
- Keep a close eye on your dog's state and interrupt the pattern of behaviour to create new patterns.

Chapter 16
Toilet Issues

Innate behaviours

In the wild, it is typically the leader wolves that mark the territory, the reason being that their scent tells other wolves their age, status and sex through the pheromones. This message communicates to other wolves that the area is occupied, and that they should stay away. This is necessary to protect their food resources and security. Although marking is considered a redundant practice, as it will not effectively serve its original purpose, the dog does not understand this. Marking behaviour is innate and dogs still receive and send many messages through doing so. I witnessed one dog mark the banister each time the doorbell rang to communicate to the person who was coming in that it was their territory.

If your dog is demonstrating an undesirable behaviour of toileting in the home, consider the reasons behind it. It may be due to a physiological need, such as needing to go but not being able to get outside, or a dog may not feel safe outside and so toilets in the home where it feels comfortable. Alternatively, the problem could be due to a health issue, such as suffering from a urinary tract disease. It can also be spurred on by confusion in belonging needs, i.e. the dog thinks it is in charge and so is instinctively marking territory, or, most commonly, it could be due to of a lack of confidence – the dog does not know where they should toilet.

Some dogs will toilet in the home soon as the guardians leave. Guardians can perceive this as the dog acting out of spite because of being left, whereas a model of needs, combined with top-down philosophy, would conclude the most likely possibility: the dog does this to leave its scent so you can smell your way back to the home. Obviously we cannot smell our way back home, but our dogs do not know this. We often anthropomorphise but they also do the equivalent: they 'canidmorphise' – attribute canine personalities to our behaviour!

Lula's story

Ben and Molly were guardians to a two-year-old Jack Russell cross named Lula. They informed me that Lula had not toileted in the home since she was a pup but in the last month, she'd had many 'accidents' and rarely toileted outside.

I arrived at Ben and Molly's home and they began to explain how frustrated they were with Lula's toileting situation, as they had been forced to pull up the carpets. Whilst they were explaining the situation, I noticed that Ben was finding it hard to look at me as he constantly had one eye on Lula, waiting to correct her in case she would toilet. I also noticed that Lula was staring right back at Ben and followed him around everywhere he went. It quickly became apparent that the more Ben was in communication with Lula by constantly looking at her, the more Lula thought Ben needed her and so followed him around.

I pointed the following out to Ben: 'Although I understand that you're looking at Lula, being worried she'll toilet on the carpet, she doesn't understand that. She just sees you looking at her with concern and misinterprets your look as meaning that you need her. As a result, she can't relax and won't leave your side.' I went on to explain how dogs can start toileting in the home at any age due to unmet needs, and how to adopt Guardian Role principles. Once the consultation was finished, Ben and Molly felt confident they could resolve the problem.

In the days that followed, Ben released his gaze from Lula, the intense communication subsided, and she began to relax. Once she understood that Ben and Molly were in charge, after a couple of corrections, she returned to toileting in the correct place.

Constant marking outside

If the dog is convinced by your leadership but still stops to sniff and mark on every tree and lamppost, it is simply an undesirable behaviour that has formed over time to become a habit. This can be annoying when you have somewhere to get to; also, as your dog is deciding where to stop, this will in turn compromise your leadership on the walk. As with addressing any behaviour, you must ensure your dog's actual needs are being/will be met, whilst demonstrating you are leader. So if your dog marks 20 times on a 10-minute walk to the park, you can safely assume they do not need to go that many times. To change this habit, aim to decrease the number of times your dog stops by a couple of times each walk; do this by continuing to move where you would normally stop. You should encourage your dog to keep moving when you see them slow down by giving the lead a gentle tug and saying 'come on'. When doing this, consider your dog's need to toilet by choosing to stop when you decide it is appropriate – which might be once or twice on a 10-minute walk. Over the days, new desirable patterns of behaviour will form.

Added tips

- Toileting in the home could be due to a medical or behavioural reason, so it is best to explore every option.
- Dogs need to feel safe and comfortable to relieve themselves. If they appear to be nervous outside, take them to a place where they are relaxed.
- For more tips on teaching your dog where to toilet, see Chapter 21 – Puppies.

Chapter 17
Nervous Behaviours

Of all the problems dogs can have, the saddest to witness are displays of nervous behaviour. Typical examples of this can range from a dog being highly alert and alarmed by everyday noises or activity, to appearing withdrawn and shut down. In these cases, the dogs are demonstrating that they cannot cope with the responsibility of being leader and desperately need someone to fulfil the role in order for their quality of life to improve.

Jodie's story

Whilst I was out walking with a dog in the park one afternoon, I began chatting to a lady named Tracy. She mentioned that she and her husband, Chris, had a rescue Whippet called Jodie, whom they were unable to bring to the park as she would become overwhelmed by the sight of too many people and would freeze and tremble. Apparently, Jodie was particularly nervous around men and would roll over and urinate if they went near her. I told Tracy about my work and she asked me to her home to see if I could help her address Jodie's nervous behaviour.

I arrived and Chris invited me in. Immediately upon seeing me, Jodie hid behind the couch. Tracy and Chris informed me that she would spend many hours there each day and would not get up for her food. I explained they had to take the pressure off by not looking at her, instead allowing her to see for herself that they were fulfilling their role as leader.

I began explaining the Guardian Role principles in detail and we didn't pay any attention to Jodie. Three hours into the consultation, she had come out from behind the couch and was sitting by Tracy. I pointed out that because we were not looking at her or making any movements towards her, as a result, we were not seen to be asking things from her. This was giving her the time and space to assess what was going on. As a result, she was slowly becoming more relaxed in her environment and my presence, and able to take in information. Tracy and Steven were surprised that she had come out from behind the couch, especially as there was a male visitor in the room.

This was progress – and however small it was, it gave Tracy and Chris something to build upon. Once I'd explained all the Guardian Role principles, they felt confident enough to address the issues and were keen to begin.

In the days that followed, they relaxed their interactions with Jodie, communicating with her only on their terms and much less often, and ensuring they never went up to her at any point. This meant that Jodie now had long, uninterrupted periods without being looked at or spoken to, which gave her the space and time to assess her environment and to see Tracy and Chris fulfilling the role of guardians. They invited many friends around to the home and instructed them not to look at or speak to Jodie. With each positive encounter with a visitor, Jodie spent less time behind the couch before coming out; she finally stopped going behind the couch altogether. Tracy then asked her visitors to call Jodie over to them for a stroke after the golden five-minute ritual, and Jodie happily obliged.

A week later, Tracy reported that Jodie was showing more confidence by playing and running around in the front room whilst they had a male visitor.

Meanwhile, Tracy and Chris continued to communicate their role outside by going out to quiet parks via quiet streets, always keeping an eye on Jodie's state. If Jodie ever appeared concerned by the presence of other people, they would choose flight by walking off in a different direction. Soon, Jodie was receiving many lessons that assured her she was being listened to and taken care of both inside the home and outside. Once she was comfortable in places with a few people present, Tracy and Chris built up to going to busier areas. Six months on from the consultation, and to this day, I often see Tracy walking in the park where we first met, with Jodie following confidently behind her.

Building confidence with dogs that suffer from nervous behaviour is one of the hardest symptoms to tackle. The dogs are so overwhelmed by their perceived problems that every sound and sight appears magnified to them. As a result, it takes much patience and planning about what experiences they are exposed to in order to avoid setbacks. When addressing nervous behaviour, many guardians have found it vital to measure the dog's progress by breaking the stages down into manageable checkpoints. This helps them to understand where they are at and how to slowly build on that.

Dogs that are scared to go into cars

An example of breaking down the stages into checkpoints can be highlighted through the process of encouraging a scared dog to get into a car. A good indication of whether or not the dog is stressed at any point is to see if they will take a food reward in that moment. If they don't, it often suggests that they are too stressed and that we should not continue.

A table illustrating stages and checkpoints to get a fearful dog into a car.

STAGE	ACTION	IS THE DOG COMFORTABLE? IF SO, MOVE TO THE NEXT CHECKPOINT.
STAGE 1	WALK A FEW METRES AWAY FROM THE CAR, AND REWARD WITH FOOD.	
STAGE 1.1	WALK A METRE AWAY FROM THE CAR, AND REWARD WITH FOOD.	
STAGE 1.2	WALK PAST THE CAR AND PUT YOUR HAND ON THE DOOR; REWARD WITH FOOD.	
STAGE 1.3	WALK TO THE CAR, OPEN THE DOOR AND CLOSE IT; REWARD WITH FOOD.	
STAGE 1.4	WALK TO THE CAR, OPEN THE DOOR, STAND THERE FOR A BRIEF TIME, AND THEN CLOSE THE DOOR; REWARD WITH FOOD.	

STAGE 1.5	WALK TO THE CAR, OPEN THE DOOR, REWARD THE DOG AND STAND THERE FOR A LONGER TIME. THEN CLOSE THE DOOR AND REWARD WITH FOOD.	
STAGE 1.6	WALK TO THE CAR AND THEN AROUND IT TO OPEN ANOTHER DOOR; REWARD WITH FOOD, THEN CLOSE THE DOOR AND WALK OFF.	
STAGE 1.7	WALK TO THE CAR, WALK AROUND IT AND OPEN THE DOORS; REWARD WITH FOOD, CLOSE THE DOORS AND THEN WALK OFF.	
STAGE 1.8	WALK TO THE CAR, SIT INSIDE WITH THE DOG OUTSIDE; REWARD WITH FOOD AND THEN GET OUT AND WALK OFF.	
STAGE 1.9	WALK TO THE CAR, SIT INSIDE, CALL THE DOG IN AND GIVE A FOOD REWARD AND PRAISE AS SOON AS IT VENTURES FORWARD. THEN GET OUT AND WALK OFF.	

STAGE 2	GET IN THE CAR, CALL THE DOG IN AND REWARD THEM, STAYING INSIDE.	
STAGE 2.1	GET IN THE CAR; TURN THE ENGINE ON AND OFF, WHILST REWARDING THE DOG.	
STAGE 3	GET IN THE CAR WITH THE DOG, TURN THE ENGINE ON, STAY THERE FOR SOME TIME THEN REWARD THE DOG.	
STAGE 3.1	GET IN THE CAR WITH THE DOG, TURN THE ENGINE ON, DRIVE OUT OF THE DRIVE AND BACK AGAIN.	
STAGE 3.2	AND SO ON.	

Added tips

- Do not rush – it takes as long as it takes.
- Do not take your dog to the point where its state heightens and it resists.

Chapter 18
Double Trouble

When a guardian has two or more dogs displaying behavioural problems, it is usually clear which one thinks it has the responsibilities of leader. A dog that thinks it is in charge is typically first on the scene, displaying a noticeable range of undesirable behaviour, with the other dog or dogs appearing to back it up in its decision. However, often, everything is not as it seems.

Rosie and Holly's story

Donna and William were the guardians to two Labradors named Rosie and Holly. Rosie and Holly were quite well-behaved, except that when they were out on a walk and sometimes saw a particular dog, they felt it necessary to warn it off. In these moments, Rosie would go to inspect the dog and Holly would follow. Once next to the other dog, Rosie's body language would become rigid (she chose the freeze response), her tail would rise, and if the dog reacted in any other way except with a submissive action such as moving away, both Rosie and Holly would tell it off with a couple of barks and some mouthing. Only when the dog had backed off would Rosie and Holly would walk on.

This behaviour never escalated to a fight, as it was intended only as a warning signal for other dogs to go away. However, Rosie and Holly's combined behaviour was clearly intimidating to other dogs and needed to be addressed. When

Donna and William were going away on holiday, they asked me to stay in their home and work on the dogs' behaviour in their absence.

To begin, I had Rosie on a long lead, enabling me to prevent her from going up to and dealing with dogs she felt needed to be warned away. It also gave me the necessary control to show both dogs that I was making the decisions for their safety by walking away before they had the chance to react.

With the few experiences we encountered each day, I was sometimes able to walk away with both dogs without an issue, but at other times, I was unsuccessful in demonstrating my role as decision-maker. In these moments, Rosie would struggle and appear frustrated that she couldn't get to the other dog, whilst Holly, who was off lead, would approach the other dog. I was finding it very hard to get across a clear message that I was protecting both of them, and I couldn't manage both on a long lead as they would become tangled, so eventually, I decided to take them out separately. Interestingly, when I did this, neither Rosie or Holly would react to other dogs, and so the opportunities to teach them became even more infrequent. Eventually, I returned to taking them both out together.

A week passed and I had still not made much progress due to the lack of opportunity and my inability to control each and every situation. This resulted in the decision to put Holly on the long lead instead of Rosie to see if it would make a difference.

The next time we were walking in the park, I saw a dog they both took a dislike to, so I marched off in the opposite direction with Holly on the long lead. Just as before, Rosie went up to the dog and froze, but without Holly there to back her up, she paused there only for a short period of time before running back to catch up with Holly and me. Once this scenario had repeated itself a number of times, I realised I should have had Holly on the long lead from the start.

It dawned on me that Holly had, in fact, been making the decisions when sighting perceived dangers this whole time. This had not been clear at first, as Rosie would always get to the dogs first because she was quicker and more impulsive. But it was Holly who made the very subtle signs that the other dog needed to be dealt with and, once she'd made a movement, Rosie would join in, making more noise, and so appearing as if she were the main instigator. There were occasions where dogs would follow Holly as we were walking off. In these moments, I would stop and greet the dog in a friendly tone before Holly could deal with them. If she tried to get in front of me to deal with the dog, I would move her away and carry on communicating as before.

In the days that followed, this dynamic became more evident, as I began to notice that Rosie would regularly look to Holly for her cues before going up to other dogs, so once I was able to influence Holly's decisions, Rosie followed in line.

Once William and Donna returned from holiday, I taught them the Guardian Role principles and how to successfully manage the situation with both dogs. They continued where I left off in order to convincingly demonstrate their leadership position to both Rosie and Holly.

In many ways, it can be harder to address infrequent misbehaviour with dogs, due to there being fewer opportunities to put in lessons. In addition, the unpredictability of the behaviour means the guardian is often not prepared to deliver a lesson convincingly. It also takes discipline to resist letting a dog off lead when it is quite well-behaved, but it is important to resist in order to accumulate the positive lessons.

Rosie and Holly taught me the importance of ensuring each lesson is a clear one by managing a situation so I have control, by delaying the gratification of letting a dog off lead until the problems are rectified, and by paying closer attention to the subtleties of canine language.

Added tips

- Make sure you have the necessary control to demonstrate your role in every situation.
- If you have more than one dog and are finding it problematic to communicate to both of them, work with each one separately before bringing them back together, whether that is in the home or outside.
- Avoid getting a second dog until the first one is well-behaved.

Chapter 19
Managing Other People

Managing your dog with other people can be a tough task at times as everyone has their own ideas about how to interact with it. However, to avoid any confusion, and speed up the process, your dog needs consistent communication with everyone it comes into contact with.

Sydney's story

Vince was the guardian to a Chihuahua named Sydney, who pulled on the lead and showed aggressive behaviour towards anyone that came near him. This was a particular problem for Vince as he ran a clothing factory and Sydney came to work with him. There were 10 other people working alongside Vince, and in addition to this, the factory was frequented by many delivery people throughout the day, which caused Sydney to go into a panic. This was becoming a real problem for Vince, as it was making him less productive at work and causing a great deal of stress.

Vince invited me into his place of work to see if I could help the situation. As soon as I arrived, Sydney began barking and following me around. I refrained from looking at or speaking to him. I explained to Vince that Sydney was attempting to deal with me as the perceived danger, and that Vince must demonstrate to Sydney that it wasn't his job. I asked Vince to move Sydney away from me each time he barked. After 10 corrections, Sydney settled down. Once

Vince had explained the problems he'd been having, I talked about the Guardian Role principles and how to apply them. Vince acknowledged that he understood what he had to do, but voiced his concern about the practicalities of doing it in the work environment, where he had a job to do and 10 people to manage. I mentioned that Sydney also believed he had a job to do and that, as far as he was concerned, lives were on the line. The only way for him to give up the role was if someone else he trusted was doing it for him.

I sensed that Vince felt overwhelmed by the task in hand so I broke it down by first asking if he thought gesture eating was going to be a problem. He didn't think it would be, so I then asked him if he was able to thank, look and isolate if Sydney barked at the deliverymen. As Vince stated he wasn't always in the office when the men arrived, I asked if Sydney could be put in the office when Vince went out. This would ensure that Sydney was not exposed to any experiences where he would feel the need to protect himself and the rest of the staff in Vince's absence.

I then explained that Vince could manage the other elements of perceived danger and status by informing people not to approach Sydney. I suggested we print out and display some posters with an image of Sydney and instructions asking delivery people and employees not to approach him at any point. Vince called his employees into the office so that I could explain how Sydney felt threatened when people approached him, and I went through the concept of golden five-minute ritual. All of Vince's team were on board and happy to do this.

Next, we went through the walk. As Vince pointed out that he paid a number of people from the office to take Sydney out, I suggested that we all go out for a walk together to teach stop, start, and change direction to Sydney, during which time, each staff member took turns teaching Sydney not to pull. After the consultation had finished, I asked Vince to keep me updated.

In the days that followed, Vince stuck rigidly to the plan. He informed me that each time someone came into the factory and Sydney barked, Vince thanked, looked and then isolated him if necessary. As a result, Sydney had calmed down in that area. In addition, staff members had stopped going up to Sydney and his walkers were all managing to take him out without him pulling on the lead. And when he was not able to put in the lessons, Vince was also remembering to keep Sydney in the office where he felt safe.

Vince managed to address the situation in a very short amount of time by ensuring that every person who came into contact with Sydney was not confusing the messages Vince was giving. Now Vince is able to productively manage his team – including Sydney.

Chapter 20
Dogs and Children

There are numerous incidents of dogs biting people every year, and most of these cases involve children. However, the vast majority of incidents can be easily avoided if the guardian manages the interaction between child and dog by following some simple rules:

1. Make sure that the child is not permitted to approach your dog when it is eating, lying on the floor/bed, on the lead or just standing around. Instead, ask the child to call the dog over for attention. If the dog wants to go over for attention, it will.

2. Make sure the child does not pull on the dog's ears or tail, poke its eyes, grab its fur or do anything else that the dog finds uncomfortable.

3. Teach the child how to stroke your dog. Stroking a dog should be done slowly and gently, starting at the side of the neck and moving to the shoulder or chest.

4. If children are playing or making noise near your dog, watch out for distress signals such as baring of teeth, licking of lips, growling, tail between legs, ears back and/or head down, walking away or yawning outside the context of waking up. In these moments, the guardian must intervene and remove the dog from the situation.

5. Never leave a dog and child in the same room without someone to supervise the behaviour of both.

6. Teach your dog to play nicely and respect your personal space and that of other adults before introducing it to children. If your dog does not invade personal space, the likelihood is that it will be the same with children.

7. Do not allow children to play tug of war with your dog. The dog may not be aware of its own strength.

Charlie's story

Charlie was a beautiful ten-month-old Cockapoo who lived with his guardians, Cassie and Paul, and their two children, Abigail and Sofia. Cassie and Paul contacted me after an incident in which one of the girls' friends had come over for a play date and was bitten by Charlie. They were extremely distraught about what had happened and desperate to address the situation.

I arrived at Paul and Cassie's home and they told me about the problems they were experiencing with Charlie. I asked what had led up to him biting the friend. Apparently, the girl had gone to cuddle Charlie, at which point, he had bitten her on the forehead and left a little mark. Since then, his behaviour had grown worse and he had progressed to growling at children at the school gate.

Whilst Cassie was talking, I noticed that Abigail and Sofia kept going up to and playing with Charlie. He looked happy enough, but nonetheless, I pointed out to Cassie and Paul that the girl had been bitten at the moment when Charlie's space was invaded, and that now the same thing was happening in front of us.

I went on to explain that although Charlie appeared confident and happy to play with the girls, there are times when a dog does not want to interact. In those moments, it was essential that Charlie was left alone, otherwise, he would express his discomfort by growling or, if that did not work, snapping. Clearly, it was too much to expect the girls or their friends to read Charlie's body language so, to ensure Charlie never felt uncomfortable, I suggested the girls get into the habit of always calling him over to interact, rather than going up to him. That way, he would be in control of whether he wanted to interact or not.

Cassie and Paul understood this but expressed concern that the children might not listen to them. I explained that, as guardians, we have no choice but to get our children to listen; if not, incidents can occur. Another bite to a child would undoubtedly result in Charlie being rehomed at best, or at worst, put to sleep. This could easily be avoided by respecting his space.

I began talking to the girls, explaining how Charlie felt when his space was invaded and demonstrating the experience by invading the girls' space, going up close to them and putting my hands near their faces. The girls laughed awkwardly but showed understanding about how Charlie might feel. I explained the status rule (golden five minutes, do not go up to the dog; invitation only with play and affection) and asked them to do this with Charlie.

I drew out a reward chart for the girls as extra incentive to follow the new regime. If the girls interacted with Charlie properly by calling him over, each day, they would get a tick in the left-hand box, which would convert to a penny. If they invaded his space, they would get a cross in the right-hand section and lose two pennies. They could get a maximum of 10 pence per day each and were each allowed to call Charlie over a maximum of 15 times per day. This ensured he would not be overly bothered by the girls and could rest.

ABIGAIL		SOFIA	
MAXIMUM 10P A DAY		MAXIMUM 10P A DAY	
CALLING CHARLIE OVER: +1P	INVADING CHARLIE'S SPACE: -2P	CALLING CHARLIE OVER: +1P	INVADING CHARLIE'S SPACE: -2P

The girls seemed enthusiastic and immediately began calling Charlie over and refrained from invading his space.

Paul commented that it would be extremely hard to manage the children at the school gates as they all tended to come over and crowd Charlie. Was it possible, I asked, to manage this situation so Charlie's space was not invaded? It seemed not, so I advised Cassie and Paul to stop taking Charlie to school to avoid any more incidents, and I also explained the Guardian Role principles.

In the days that followed, the girls stuck to the new rules. Occasionally, they would get it wrong but as soon as they saw Cassie or Paul put a cross on the chart, they were keen to avoid making the same mistake.

Furthermore, Cassie and Paul educated every child who visited in how to interact with Charlie. They also never left Charlie and the children in the same room unattended. With each day that passed, Cassie and Paul's confidence grew, as it became clear that Charlie was comfortable in the company of children. Likewise, Charlie's confidence that children were not a threat was growing with each correct interaction.

A few weeks after the consultation, I got a call from Cassie explaining that a child had run up to pet Charlie whilst they were out on the walk. Cassie told me she managed to quickly position herself in front of Charlie to stop his space being invaded. This quick reaction ensured Charlie felt protected and prevented an incident occurring. Cassie went on to say that Charlie did not look fazed by the event but said she would never take any chances.

It was great to hear that Cassie had been able to react appropriately. Cassie and Paul were doing what all great guardians do; rather than expecting Charlie to accept his space being intruded and punishing him when he did not conform, they were working with their dog's nature, communicating their role clearly and managing each situation effectively.

Introducing your dog to your newborn

Introducing your dog to your newborn can be a daunting experience, not least due to the worry about how the dog will take to the baby. Here are instructions to ensure the introduction goes smoothly.

1. Make sure the dog understands that you are leader before planning/having a baby. This will ensure that your dog is calm, responsive to your requests and does not feel responsible for the wellbeing of others.
2. When bringing the baby home for the first time, have your dog in another room. This will allow you to get settled before introducing them to each other. Once settled, ask your partner to put your dog on its lead and bring it into the room at a good distance from you and the baby.
3. Go through the golden five-minute ritual. This gives the dog time to calm and observe the baby from a distance. If the dog becomes excited and attempts to invade your space (which is unlikely if instructional

point 1 is achieved), ask your partner to isolate the dog.

4. Once the dog is calm with you and the baby in the room, you can sit down on the couch with your baby. Here, you can calmly chat to each other to show the dog you are relaxed. If your dog looks relaxed, ask your partner to come closer. The key here is to make sure the dog is calm before moving forward. If the dog's state heightens, move back or put the dog in the other room. Once your dog is calm around the baby, you can let it off lead.

5. If your baby cries and your dog reacts, calmly remove it from the situation and do not make a big deal of it. If you panic, you will make something out of nothing. Rather, be calm and manage the introduction in baby steps.

Added tips

- It does not matter how cute the breed is or how good a dog's temperament might be – all dogs are capable of biting if they are stressed and feel threatened.
- If you feel your child will not listen to you and is constantly encroaching on your dog's space, serious consideration of rehoming your dog is required. Rehoming a dog before an incident occurs is the kindest thing to do in the long run.

Chapter 21
Puppies

If you are getting a puppy, your time together will be both a joyful and challenging experience. Joyful because there is nothing quite like watching a beautiful, loving bundle of energy explore the home, play and give you affection. And challenging because of the problems that typically occur, such as toileting in the home, separation anxiety, overly excitable behaviour, nipping and much more. In this chapter, I aim to answer the most common puppy-related questions.

Where should I get a puppy?

There are many responsible breeders who have the dog's welfare at heart and whose primary concern is producing healthy dogs with good temperaments. Unfortunately, there is also a huge rise in puppy farming, which needs to be avoided at all costs as it is a business that does not care for a dog's welfare but is there to simply make money. This means that the breeding dog and her puppies are kept in terrible conditions, which is not only cruel for the breeding dog but in turn, may likely affect the puppies' crucial first eight weeks of development.

To avoid buying from a puppy farm, don't buy a puppy:

- From a person who breeds from more than two breeds of dog, or has multiple litters at the same time.

- Unless you are allowed to visit the breeder's home and can see the mother of the puppy.
- If the dogs or puppies do not look healthy and the living conditions do not appear satisfactory.
- From a breeder that would refuse to take the puppy back in the event of an unexpected problem.
- If the breeder insists you take the puppy before it is eight weeks old.

Bringing the puppy home

Once you have brought the puppy home, make sure it has:
- Access to water all day.
- Food – puppies typically need feeding three to four times a day.
- A relaxing environment – it is best to start off restricting the puppy's environment to one or two rooms. This will ensure they do not become overwhelmed exploring their environment, and give them the necessary time to rest.
- Access to an appropriate spot to toilet.
- A comfy bed.
- Nothing around that it can chew that could potentially harm it.
- A toy it can chew on – puppies have an overwhelming urge to chew, so protect your furniture by giving them something they can chew on.
- Plenty of company.

How do I teach my dog to toilet outside?

Start by keeping an eye on your dog's signs that they are about to go. This could range from sniffing or whining, to circling and lowering its hind legs. You should also be aware of the times your dog typically needs to go and lead it to the designated area. This could be a few minutes after it has had a drink or some food, or after it has just woken up. When you see your dog squatting in the correct place, say a word or short phrase so it associates the action with your request – for example, 'be quick' – and give it a treat to reinforce the good behaviour. Over time, if you repeat this phrase with the action, your dog will learn to associate toileting with your request. Avoid saying 'good girl/boy' when your dog toilets, as you may say this phrase later using the same body language and tonality in the home, with unwanted consequences.

If your dog gets it wrong by toileting in the incorrect place then clean it up with a pet odour eliminator without saying a word. In these moments, it is extremely important not to get frustrated or angry, or to move erratically, as this will likely frighten your dog and it may then become fearful of going to the toilet near you. If you see that your dog is about to go, you can gently and calmly move it to the designated spot to show where it should be going.

Management

If you are puppy toilet training and you live in a flat, making it difficult to get outside in time, or if you do not have a garden/outside area, it will help to purchase some toilet training mats. This way, you can start off teaching your puppy to toilet on the training mats and build up to going in a desired location once their bladders increase in size. To manage the exercise, have a toilet training mat in each room. Keep all the doors closed so your puppy is in your sight and close to a mat. Once your puppy learns to toilet on the mats, you can reduce how many are in the home until you eventually remove them all when it is toileting outside. You can further manage the home by picking up rugs and covering carpets whilst toilet training your dog.

To crate or not to crate?

Whilst in a crate, a puppy will commonly hold its bladder. Not in all cases, mind you, but the majority do. This can prove useful in managing the situation whilst you are out of the room by avoiding any unwanted stains on your carpet, and will also maximise toilet training lessons. However, some puppies find being locked in a crate very traumatic. This can be addressed by making it a more desirable place to go: keep the door open, make it comfy, and associate the experience with something positive, like receiving treats. Once the puppy likes being in the crate, close the door for short amounts of time and open it before it has a chance to whine. The time the puppy is left in the crate can then be slowly built up so that your puppy never becomes distressed. This exercise can take time and effort so it is advisable to only purchase a crate if you really need one.

How can I get my puppy to settle at nighttime?

Being left on its own all night can be a distressing experience for a puppy. To prepare for this, first ensure that the puppy is familiar with you leaving the room and returning during the day by walking in and out again whilst adopting the golden five-minute ritual. If your dog reacts with severe separation anxiety, refer to Chapter 12.

To address the first couple of nights, it is a kind action to sleep close to your puppy so they get a chance to settle into their new surroundings. You could sleep on the couch or set up a temporary bed close to where they sleep. After a night or two, your puppy will be more relaxed in the home and no doubt you will want to get back to your bed. To achieve this, do not say anything upon leaving the puppy in its sleeping place; just turn out the light and go. Do not worry if your puppy whines a little when you leave, as this is natural behaviour. However, if it becomes very stressed and starts whining loudly, enter the room to show them you are still in the home and they are safe, but don't say anything to them. Whilst you are in the room, you can check to see if your puppy has toileted. If it has, clean it up without saying anything and then leave.

You can repeat this several times for the first night – say, five times – but after that, do not go in again (providing you know your puppy's needs are met). If your puppy still whines the next night, you can enter the room in the same fashion. But this time, only go back in four times, and then decrease this number by one on each of the following nights. This will allow your puppy to accept its sleeping place and feel safe in the knowledge they are not alone.

How do I stop my puppy nipping?

When pups nip each other, they get a mouth full of fur. However, we have only skin, so a puppy's sharp teeth can hurt. To discourage the behaviour, make sure that, from the outset, you are dictating when to interact/play with the puppy.

If your puppy nips you, redirect the behaviour by giving them something they can bite and chew such as a toy. The chewing allows them to soothe their mouths when they are teething. If the puppy ignores the toy and comes back to nip you again, look in a different direction and gently push it away, giving it a clear signal to say their behaviour is not welcome. If it persists on nipping you, the next step is to move the puppy away completely. If it comes back again, you should isolate it in another room for a very short time so it realises the consequence of its actions, all without speaking or looking. Once you let your puppy out, go back to what you were doing. If your puppy's nipping persists then repeat the isolation whilst slowly building up the time.

Puppies can be quite tenacious with nipping, so show them you are more tenacious by not giving up, whilst all the time staying calm.

How do I stop my puppy running around the house?

Every puppy has a funny five minutes or more at least once a day. During this time, they may run up and down the home at great speed, playing with their toys. This is a puppy's natural behaviour so, as long as your puppy is not nipping, damaging objects or invading anyone's space, leave them to it.

When does a puppy need its injections?

Mother's milk contains natural immunity for her puppies; this wears off after six to eight weeks. It is typically between six and ten weeks old that puppies get immunisation through two vaccinations, so ask your breeder what injections your puppy has already had and then book in to see your vet.

Microchipping

Microchipping your dog is compulsory in England, Northern Ireland, Wales, New Zealand, Japan and parts of Australia. In countries where it is not compulsory, it is still advised to do so in case your pet goes missing. Microchipping involves inserting a tiny microchip in the loose skin of the dog's neck and back; this is done by your vet. Your contact details will be on the microchip, enabling your dog to be identified by a shelter, other vets and dog wardens if it is found. Ensure you update your address and other details on the database if you move.

When can I take my puppy outside?

Most vets advise to wait a week after the second injection before taking your puppy outside the home, but some advise two weeks. Consult your vet to hear their opinion.

How much exercise does my puppy need each day?

As puppies' bones are soft as they are still growing, too much exercise can harm them. A general rule is five minutes' exercise a day per each month of age (up to twice a day). So if your puppy is three months old, that is two fifteen-minute walks. Once puppies have fully grown, they can handle more exercise, depending on the breed.

Should I use a lead and collar or a harness?

I have been using a lead and collar since I began working with dogs, but have recently had a change of thinking. Not because I have seen any evidence that a lead and collar causes damage to a dog's neck, but because I believe people when they say it potentially could. To remove all doubt, if your dog pulls a lot, use a lead and harness (one that does not restrict your dog's walking motion) so you can correct it without placing pressure on the neck. If your dog does not pull, a lead and collar will be fine. A harness is especially necessary for puppies that pull.

Chilli's story

A lady named Henrietta called me for help because she was struggling to cope with her 13-week-old rescue puppy called Chilli. Chilli would toilet in the home each time, missing the training mats. Henrietta was concerned her carpet was being ruined so she resorted to taking Chilli outside to toilet on a patch of grass, which was 40 metres from the home. This was becoming a real burden for her, as Chilli often needed to go to the toilet. She added that in the last week, Chilli had refused to walk so she had been carrying him. In addition, Chilli had started biting both her and the children whenever they went to pick him up to go outside.

Henrietta was so stressed with his toileting and the work involved that she was considering returning Chilli to the rescue centre. It was sad to hear Henrietta's frustration at how unmanageable the situation was, and even sadder to think that Chilli could potentially be going back to a rescue centre for a second time, especially being so young.

I arrived at Henrietta's home and she began talking me through the problems she was experiencing with Chilli. The knock-on effect of problems that were occurring due to not being able to get Chilli to toilet on the mats soon became apparent. Chilli refused to go on the walk, I explained, because he was scared of going outside and no one had been picking up on his efforts to communicate this, which had resulted in him making the message clearer by biting anyone who went to pick him up to take him.

Henrietta said she had no choice, as Chilli wouldn't toilet on the mats and needed a walk. I explained that, with perseverance, he would learn to toilet on the mats and that walks were not as important as his need to feel safe. I first addressed how to toilet train and manage the home by putting down a protective cover on the carpet, reducing access to other rooms and providing more training mats, as Henrietta's front room was larger than average.

I then asked Henrietta to come outside with me. We sat outside and concentrated on all the noise and sights around us, and it became very clear just how much was going on. I explained that, as human beings, we filter out many of the noises because we can identify what they are and know we are safe; however, Chilli couldn't do this yet, so each sound and sight was amplified. Every time he was taken out, he felt as if he were being put in danger.

Henrietta understood and agreed not to take him out until he was ready. From then on, she concentrated on toilet training by getting Chilli to go on the mats and communicating her role inside the home. Once the protective sheets were down and Henrietta wasn't taking Chilli out, the situation relaxed. After two weeks of toilet training, Chilli was going on the mat every time. Henrietta then worked on making sure his experience outside was short and enjoyable by going out only for a brief moment and then coming back in. During the time outside, she would use praise and treats. Gradually, the time going out was built up and Henrietta and her children chose to walk on the quieter streets, moving to the busier streets only when it was clear that Chilli was ready. Now Chilli does not bite anyone or refuse to go on walks; in fact, he loves going out!

My experience with Henrietta and Chilli reinforced the message of just how important it is to understand the dog's needs in each moment. I recall another case where a couple and their three children were so excited at getting a puppy that they were constantly playing with her and giving her attention. They also had many visits from their neighbours and friends who wanted to see the puppy. This puppy became so overtired from the constant interaction that she resorted to biting the family members and visitors in an attempt to communicate she wanted to be left alone to rest. In scenarios such as these, guardians will seek out dog trainers to address the behaviour but so often, if they have a clear understanding of their dog's needs in the first place, these behaviours would not occur.

Chapter 22
A Realisation

"Dogs do speak, but only to those who know how to listen." (Orhan Pamuk)

For a period of time in my younger years, I was unaware of how to care for or communicate with dogs. I made many mistakes, such as simply assuming they understood my role as their guardian without communicating it. I also placed them in situations, not understanding what their needs were. My lack of knowledge, combined with my poor judgement, resulted in events I am ashamed to share with you. But I believe it is necessary to tell the following story in the hope that others may avoid making similar mistakes.

Blake's story

I was the guardian to a beautiful German Shepherd called Blake. When Blake was a puppy, we had a morning ritual of going out to a grass area at the front of my home so he could have a run, play and go to the toilet. After he had relieved himself and played for some time, I would call him to me and we would go back inside.

One day, when Blake was a little older, he refused to come to me when called. Instead, he pranced around me as if to instigate a game of chase. I kept calling him but he continued with his antics. I tried to grab him but he was too fast to catch and so, after a few unsuccessful minutes of trying to get hold of him, I changed tactic by throwing a stick on the ground. Once he stopped to investigate the stick, I was able to grab hold of him and then walk him back into the home.

The next day, we went through our usual ritual. Again, after Blake had played for some time, he would not come when I called him. Instead, he ran circles around me and barked. I tried the same distraction technique as the previous day. However, this time, although I had not learnt from previous experience, Blake had, and he was wise to my tactic. After many attempts to get him to come back to me to no avail, I came to the thinking that I needed to catch him in order to reprimand him for his behaviour. This way, he would understand the consequence of his actions. After 10 arduous minutes, I managed to catch him. I then walked him back into the home whilst telling him off for disobeying me.

The following day, Blake and I went out again. I let him off the lead, assuming he would have learnt a lesson from the previous day. But it soon became apparent that he had not. Instead, this time, Blake had upped his game of prancing around and was even quicker in avoiding me catching him. I quickly interpreted his actions as a lack of respect and challenge to my authority, rather than accepting what it was actually about – Blake was simply communicating that he wanted me to play, and my attempts to catch him were in fact encouraging his behaviour. I was becoming increasingly frustrated as I had things to do. Fifteen minutes went by and my frustration turned to anger. Eventually, I managed to grab hold of him, and did so with force. Blake yelped to let me know I was hurting him. I ignored him and maintained my tight grip. I marched him into the home and shouted at him to get into his bed. Blake lay in his bed looking frightened, occasionally getting out to come up to me, seeking reassurance of our friendship, but I ignored his pleas and continued to punish him by raising my voice each time and pushing him away with force when he came near. The whole experience felt horrible at the time, but I thought it was necessary to express my anger in order to communicate the message that his previous behaviour was not acceptable.

The following day, I was confident he would have learnt from this unpleasant experience so I let him off outside again. However, when I called him, he once again pranced about and ran circles around me. I was dumbfounded as to why he was doing this, and the anger flooded back. I'd had enough, and was not going to waste any more time trying to catch or distract him. So I immediately marched towards the house. Blake watched me walk off for 10 seconds before choosing to follow me.

As I entered the home, I felt relieved Blake had followed me, but soon, I became overwhelmed with guilt. Guilt, because at that point, I realised I had achieved the desired result without punishment or intimidation – and so my behaviour over the last two days had succeeded only in working myself into a heightened state and jeopardising my relationship with Blake.

My story

"A person wants to feel safe or in control, but will only give up control once they feel safe." (David Brooks)

The way I responded to Blake's undesirable behaviour was, in truth, consistent with my attitude at that time in my life. I thought that the world owed me something, and when things did not work out exactly how I planned, I became frustrated, impatient and angry. This led to many conflicts, but I could never see that I was part of the problem. Unfortunately for

Blake, he found himself at the end of my ignorance and shortcomings.

Blake's response to my behaviour, however, acted as a powerful wake-up call to some much needed self-awareness. It made me reflect on my actions and accept full responsibility for what had happened.

I was determined not to allow such a situation to occur again, so I sought to get a better understanding of dog behaviour by reading books, attending talks and enrolling on courses. I soon became inspired by the study of canine behaviour. It was as if a world previously unknown to me had suddenly been revealed. And it made complete sense to me. It was this revelation that prompted me to become a professional dog behaviourist.

Although I studied many different theories on how to communicate with dogs, it was only through working with dogs themselves that my communication skills honed and developed into successful tools for my profession: if I rushed the dogs' nurture or communicated incorrectly, they would mirror my mistakes by challenging me in multiple ways. If I identified their needs, communicated with them calmly and managed the environment, the correct bond formed and I would see their behaviour improve.

Whilst I was striving to address problem behaviours in dogs, I was inadvertently learning many lessons in leadership. In turn, this had a profound effect on my wellbeing. As I strove to identify a dog's needs in each moment, I became more aware of my own needs and how to fulfil them. As I learnt to be calm, convincing and consistent with dogs, the same occurred in my relationships with people. Once I took responsibility for everything that went wrong when working with dogs, the same occurred in my personal life. And, after some time in the company of dogs, my overall demeanour became more relaxed, confident and patient. My emotional intelligence grew and I became a happier person. The study of how to help dogs was packed full of practical ideas that helped my own life, such as learning confidence in stages, using methods to reduce state, interrupting negative patterns of behaviour to create positive patterns, setting goals, overcoming limiting beliefs and controlling one's thoughts.

I was so inspired by the life lessons I had learnt from working with dogs that I wanted to see if I could replicate the results with others through the same process. So I created a social enterprise named The Wolf Within, aimed at teaching young people with behavioural issues in pupil referral units (education systems for children who have been excluded from mainstream schools) how to help dogs with behavioural issues. I believed if I could use the study of the wolf as a metaphor to teach the young people about needs, language, state and leadership in order to overcome domestic dogs' problem behaviour, it could result in the same positive change that I had experienced.

In similar ways to dogs, the students with whom I worked displayed a variety of problem behaviours, which were very often used to compensate for their unmet needs and/or because they did not recognise their teachers as an authority. They would walk off, ignore, shut down, talk over the teachers, swear, fight with one another, and regularly reach a heightened state. However, the teachers did not react with distraction or intimidation. Rather, they sought to fulfil their needs for the teaching process to be effective: much like the desirable teaching approach for dogs. This began by providing breakfast and making sure the students had access to water, as they often came into school both hungry and thirsty. The teachers worked to provide an environment in which the students were not controlled and so were free to express themselves. They had to know how to reprimand undesirable behaviour in order for the students to think about their actions and so want to behave appropriately the next time. The teachers would then work with the students at their own pace to build their confidence. Once the students trusted the teachers, their protective barriers dropped and they became receptive to learning.

This was a process that took much time and attention – hence the PRU trying out my course in hopes of speeding up the process. The course resonated with many of the students as they had a natural empathy with animals. Through working with the dogs, they discovered that their own natures were not bad; rather, it was their experiences, and being misunderstood in particular, that had shaped their negative behaviours. And that all of them could go on to enjoy happy, peaceful lives with some careful guidance and attention. A lesson in life that all confused young people need to intrinsically know and continue to nurture.

Natural relationships

"Look deep into nature, and then you will understand everything better." (Albert Einstein)

As mentioned at the beginning of the book, there are many different theories on how to approach the dog's nurture, so I hope the Guardian Role principles resonate with you; after all (as also mentioned), they resemble those of parents raising children – except, of course, they differ in the way they're achieved.

A sure recipe to ruin a child is to misunderstand its needs or to allow it to feel responsible for fulfilling them; to let it dictate what and when it eats; to let it believe it makes the decisions regarding its safety needs. To allow it to think it can manoeuvre you anytime it wants and can dictate where and when it goes. To expose the child to too much too soon, despite its state being heightened and having a lack of confidence in a situation. And once behavioural issues arise from any of these factors then to address them by distracting the child by putting it front of the TV, controlling it with force or intimidation, or over-stimulating it by constantly trying to entertain it. And when these tactics do not work in the long term, to put it down to the child's characteristics and labelling it 'un-teachable', as opposed to constantly questioning both your leadership approach and what the child really needs from you. Yet, as tragic as this sounds, this is commonplace with how we nurture our dogs.

The Guardian Role, like good parenting, is not a quick-fix method you do for a couple of weeks. It must be continuously employed to ensure your relationship is based on clear communication, trust and understanding to form the correct attachment.

I suspect that many years ago, a correct attachment between guardian and dog would have naturally formed unconsciously, through our daily actions. This would have been due to both human and dog sharing an uncertainty about environment and so behaviours would have aligned. If there were food around, it would have been limited, so we would have had priority over what we wanted and the dogs would have had what was left. If our dog barked to alert us to danger, we would have taken its actions seriously and investigated what they were barking at. If we separated from our family, we would have greeted our human members before our canine friends and we wouldn't have pandered to the dog's advances. When it was time to hunt, it was we humans who would have instigated it. As we have become increasingly disconnected with our natural environment, in turn, we have become disconnected with dogs.

Looking into a top-down study reminds us of the canine's needs, nature and nurture, and how they have coped without us for over four million years. And with some adapting, how we can use that information to ensure that our dogs thrive in our modern-day society.

Lessons from nature

Our relationship with wolves has, for a long time, been a turbulent one, due to the fact that we were (and in some regions still are) competing for the same food. Many years ago, when we began farming livestock, the wolf saw an opportunity in targeting this weaker species of animal, which was much safer than risking their lives taking down wild prey. Consequently, they became a threat to our livelihoods and we declared war on their species. The eradication of wolves began and they lost 90 per cent of their natural habitat, with alarming consequences.

Take what happened in Yellowstone National Park as an example: the last wolf was killed there during the 1920s and Yellowstone was then left with the coyote and the bear as top predators. But the coyote was not strong or big enough to take down the adult elk, and the bear was not quick enough; this resulted in an abundance of elk. A theory suggests that a rise in elk numbers resulted in them trampling on the native flora such as cottonwood and willow, which just so happened to be the beaver's main food source. This resulted in the beaver population decreasing in Yellowstone.

In 1995, wolves were experimentally reintroduced to Yellowstone National Park. In just eight years of wolf rehabilitation, this move had a much more significant effect than predicted: as the wolves targeted elk as their primary food source, the elks' feeding habits changed to avoid areas where wolf packs settle to bring up pups, such as by streams. As a result, elk stopped trampling on the beavers' main food source, leading to a rise in the native flora. This meant the beaver population grew, resulting in more dams being built, which had the knock-on effect of changing the directions of streams and an increase in fish, birds, muskrats and waterfowl. Reintroducing wolves to their natural ecosystem had produced a complex chain reaction that allowed nature to flourish. Simply put, this natural key predator had a profound effect on the ecosystem.

On closer inspection, it is not just the wolf's family life and pack dynamics that can teach us about our domestic dogs' behaviour – and indeed, our own behaviour – but also its role in nature's ecosystem. There are many lessons we can learn from this wonderful species. We just need to learn to look and listen.

Afterword

I hope you have found this book to be informative and engaging. If you adopt the Guardian Role principles, I assure you, it will better your relationship with your dog.

Bonus videos

On purchasing this book, you get exclusive access to the accompanying bonus video tutorials, which have been uploaded on my website. The videos are designed to give you further help in visual form with step-by-step instructions demonstrating how to address problems in dogs that:

- Are fussy around food
- Bark at the door
- Show aggression to other dogs
- Jump up/invade personal space
- And pull on the lead.

Just go to 'buy the book' section on my website (http://thedogguardian.com/book) and type in your email and the password: Guardian Role.

I have no doubt that reading this book and watching the videos will bring up new questions regarding your dog's behaviour. If you go to my Facebook or YouTube page and let me know which behavioural issues you would like extra help with, I will answer the most frequently asked questions via video and upload them to the bonus videos section on the website for you to see.

Courses

If you would like to continue your journey to learn more about dogs, I also host group courses in the UK and other parts of the globe (please see website for details of upcoming events). Here, we'll explain the method in more detail whilst giving you the opportunity to talk about your own unique situation in person. If you're not able to make it there then it's no problem; I have also produced online courses with interactive questions and videos so you can learn more, wherever you are in the world.

I hope to hear from you very soon.

Best wishes,

Nigel

Acknowledgements

I have to firstly acknowledge the invaluable mentoring from Jan Fennell and Tony Knight, who taught me the language of canines. Then there were the lessons learned from watching Monty Roberts in action, the hours spent on the study of nature and wolves, examining Maslow's Hierarchy of Needs, and the endless other tools and methods I have picked up along the way by researching the wealth of knowledge already out there. And, of course, there are the lessons each and every dog has taught me, all of which have contributed to the ethos of *The Dog Guardian*.

I also wish to thank Sarah Osborne, who helped me on my journey by letting me stay on her sofa when I first started my dog-behaviour venture in London; Tony Cowell, who talked through the concept with me and helped me in many ways when I started writing this book; my parents, for being a financial rock when things were tight; Professor Luigi Boiatani, for his feedback on the first four chapters of my book; and many others who have helped me on my way, including Emma Priest, Stephanie Rutherford, Alex Brammall, and Sean Lovell for filming and editing the accompanying videos.

References

Abrantes, R. (2010). *Dog Language*. Revised ed. Wakan Tanka Publishers.

Abrantes, R. (1997). *The Evolution of Social Canine Behaviour*. Wakan Tanka Publishers.

Aloff, B. (2009). *Canine Body Language*. Dogwise Publishing.

Anchor, S. (2011). *The Happiness Advantage*. Virgin Books.

Becker, K. (2010). *Cushing's Disease: The Incurable Disease Your Vet is Likely to Miss*. [online] Healthy Pets with Dr Karen Becker. Available at: http://healthypets.mercola.com/sites/healthypets/archive/2010/09/21/cushings-disease-caused-by-pet-stress.aspx

Busch, R. H. (2009). *The Wolf Almanac*. Revised ed. The Lyons Press.

Coppinger, R. (2001). *Dogs*. Prentice Hall & IBD.

Darwin, C. (1859). *On the Origin of Species*. John Murray.

Derr, M. (2013). *How the Dog Became a Dog*. Gerald Duckworth & Co. Ltd.

Farquhar, B. *Wolf Reintroduction Changes Ecosystem*. [online] Yellowstone. Available at: http://www.yellowstonepark.com/wolf-reintroduction-changes-ecosystem/

Fennell, J. (2010). *The Dog Listener*. 10th anniversary ed. Harper.

Fennell, J. (2005). *The Seven Ages of a Dog*. HarperCollins.

Fogle, B. (1995). *The Encyclopedia of the Dog*. Dorling Kindersley Publishers Ltd.

Fogle, B. (1992). *The Dog's Mind*. Pelham Books.

Frost, J. (2006). *Supernanny*. Hodder & Stoughton.

Glover, R. and Spencer, C. (2010). *Why Does My Dog Do That?*. Self-published.

Hare, B. and Woods, V. (2013). *The Genius of Dogs*. Dutton Adult.

King, P. W. (2011). *Climbing Maslow's Pyramid*. Matador.

Lonsdale, T. (2001) *Raw Meaty Bones*. Rivetco Pty Ltd.

Mate, G. (2010). *In the Realm of Hungry Ghosts*. North Atlantic Books.

Mech, L. D. and Boitani, L. (2007). *Wolves: Behaviour, Ecology, and Conservation*. New ed. University of Chicago Press.

Miklosi, A. (2008). *Dog Behaviour, Evolution and Cognition*. Oxford University Press.

Milne, E. (2007). *The Truth About Cats and Dogs*. Book Guild Ltd.

Naisbitt, J. (1982). [online] National Library Board; original source *Megatrends*. Available at: http://www.nlb.gov.sg/sure/drowning-in-information-but-starved-for-know

Neufeld, G. *Does Your Child Have an Alpha Complex*. [online] Neufeld Institute. Available at: http://neufeldinstitute.org/does-your-child-have-an-alpha-complex/

Neufeld, G. (2006). *Hold on to Your Kids*. Reprint ed. Ballantine Books.

PBS.org, (2011). *Dogs That Changed the World: What caused the domestication of wolves?* [online] Available at: http://www.pbs.org/wnet/nature/dogs-that-changed-the-world-what-caused-the-domestication-of-wolves/1276/

Purcell, B. (2010). *Dingoes*. CSIRO Publishing.

Robbins, T. (2001). *Awaken the Giant Within*. New ed. Simon & Schuster.

Robbins, T. (2002). *Lessons in Mastery* (CD format). Abridged ed. Simon & Schuster.

Roberts, M. (2001). *Horse Sense for People*. New ed. HarperCollins.

Roberts, M. (1997). *The Horse Whisperer*. New ed. Arrow.

Rugaas, T. (2005). *On Talking Terms With Dogs*. Dogwise Publishing.

Sacks, B. N., Brown, S. K., Stephens, D., Pedersen, N. C., Wu, J. and Berry, O. (2013). *Y chromosone analysis of dingoes and Southeast Asian village dogs suggests a Neolithic continental expansion from Southeast Asia followed by multiple Austronesian dispersals*. [online] Oxford Journals: Molecular Biology and Evolution. Available at: http://mbe.oxfordjournals.org/content/early/2013/02/13/molbev.mst027.abstract

Shaw, G. B.

Shelbourne, T. (2012). *The 'Truth' About Wolves and Dogs*. Hubble and Hattie.

Taylor, J. D. (2006). *Black Bears*. Fitzhenry & Whiteside.

Thom. (2002). *All behaviour serves a purpose*. [online] CYC-Online. Available at: http://www.cyc-net.org/cyc-online/cycol-0502-editor.html

Wolfe, A. and Weston, C. (2007). Evans Mitchell Books.

Zeveloff, S. I. and Dewitte, E. (2002). *Racoons*. Smithsonian Books.

39992484R00142

Made in the USA
Middletown, DE
30 January 2017